MUSHROOM

CULTIVATION

12 WAYS TO BECOME THE MACGYVER OF MUSHROOMS

RICHARD BRAY

1st Edition, published in 2021
© 2021 by Monkey Publishing
Monkey Publishing
Lerchenstrasse 111
22767 Hamburg
Germany

Published by *Monkey Publishing*
Edited by *Lily Marlene Booth*
Cover Design by *Diogo Lando*
Cover Image by *Brkati Krokodil/Stocksy United*
Graphics on Title & Publisher Page:
Mis-Tery, Irina Skalaban/Shutterstock.com
Printed by *Amazon**

ISBN: 978-1798517772

MONKEY
PUBLISHING

OUR HAND-PICKED
BOOK SELECTION FOR YOU.

LEARN
SOMETHING NEW
EVERYDAY.

YOUR FREE BONUS

As a small token of thanks for buying this book, I am offering a free bonus gift exclusive to my readers. In this bonus book you will learn everything about mushroom farming.

Gourmet mushrooms are booming in popularity among chefs and home cooks. They attract a great price for the space and time needed to grow them, making mushroom-growing quite a profitable business compared to other crops. In the USA, Oyster and Shiitake mushrooms are selling for $10-12 per pound on the retail market. Wholesale, they sell for around $6/pound. If you have the time, energy, and commitment, it can be a very lucrative side hobby or full-time business.

So, if you want to learn more about how to make money with mushrooms you can download the free bonus here: ***https://mushroom.gr8.com***

TABLE OF CONTENTS

GRAPHIC PREVIEW

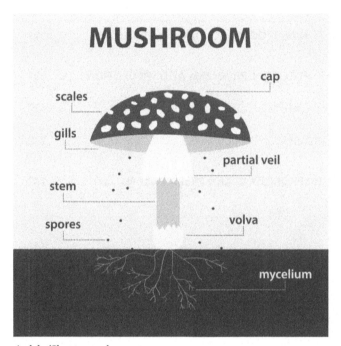

Ardelv/Shutterstock.com

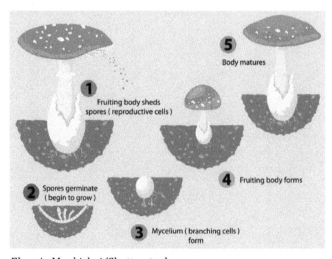

Eknarin Maphichai/Shutterstock.com

CHAPTER 1:

INTRODUCTION TO MUSHROOMS

The world of fungi is exciting and often times downright incredible. When we think of mushrooms, it is often about the few species that we find in the grocery store. These generally look similar and have the basic gills, cap, and stem and are usually brown in color. This is just one small iteration of the mushroom world, however. Mushrooms come in such a wide array of colors, shapes, and sizes that it can be entirely overwhelming. There is a whole genus of mushrooms that don't have gills at all. There are mushrooms that are bright orange, bright yellow, and vivid purple. The giant puffball mushroom (*Calvatia gigantea*) looks like a massive volleyball.

Picture 1: Giant Puffball Mushroom. PJ photography/Shutterstock.com

Mushrooms can grow on trees, on the ground, attached to dead logs, on the sides of cliffs, in the middle of forests, and in swamps. The world of mushrooms is commonly referred to as a kingdom because there are so many species and subspecies that populate the earth. I mention all this variety to give you an idea of how enormous the mushroom world is and to hopefully get you excited to enter into it. There is so much out there and so much still being discovered. Home cultivation of mushrooms is still a relatively new enterprise and techniques are being honed and developed even as I write this. Their unique and complex structures made cultivation difficult and there wasn't much success until the 17th and 18th centuries. Compared to animals and vegetables, which we began cultivating many thousands of years ago, the home-growing of mushrooms is in its infancy. This is what makes it so intriguing!

Picture 2: Mushrooms Growing on Log. Margaret Weir/Unsplash.com

Picture 3: Mushrooms Growing on Tree. Amy Humphries/Unsplash.com

Picture 4: Mushrooms Growing on Cliff. John Peel/Unsplash.com

Picture 5: Mushroom Growing on Ground. Lum3n/Unsplash.com

THE AMAZING MUSHROOM

Over 20,000 varieties of mushrooms are known in the world today, with more being discovered all the time. It is thought there are between 50,000-100,000 more varieties that haven't been found or identified. There are edible varieties, like the ones we talk about growing in the guide. There are toxic varieties, medicinal and psychoactive mushrooms, and a weird, wide, wondrous world in between.

The largest living organism *in the world* is thought to be a honey mushroom fungus in Oregon, USA. There is uncertainty as to whether it is all one organism; however, even if it is not, it is incredible in size and area. It spans 2,200 acres, is estimated to weigh 605 tons, and is around 2,400 years old.

Oyster mushrooms are making many scientists excited because of their potential use in bioremediation. Bioremediation is the breaking down or consuming of environmental pollution through the use of natural microorganisms. Oyster mushrooms might just be the key to solving the world's pollution problems! There is much still to be investigated but the research is very promising.

Another new use for mushrooms has shown up recently; using a blend of certain types to make a faux leather. There is nothing on the market yet, however several companies are showing great promise. Mushroom leather will be considerably more economically friendly than animal leather.

BENEFITS OF GROWING MUSHROOMS

Before the techniques of home cultivating were developed, people relied on foragers to provide wild mushrooms. Foraged mushrooms are wonderful and there is a large variety of species available in the wild.

The downsides to foraged mushrooms are many, however. It is almost impossible to control or even predict the yields year by year. So much depends on the weather and any fluctuations can mean no harvest at all. It is also difficult to ensure peak quality. Mushroom patches need to be watched closely because many of Mother Nature's creatures adore mushrooms as much as humans do. Bugs, rodents, and large animals alike have their favorite mushroom species and if they get to the patch before you it is all over.

One big upside to growing mushrooms, as opposed to the vegetables or flowers that people usually grow, is that there isn't any need to water or weed them. In general, once the substrate is inoculated, it is simply a waiting game. Very little time is needed to care for them, which makes them a low-effort product; perfect if you don't have tons of time on your hands! There does need to be careful attention paid to temperature and climate to make growing conditions optimal, however, so that is something that needs consideration.

HOW DO MUSHROOMS GROW?

Growing mushrooms is vastly different than growing most other plants or vegetables. They have no seeds. Instead, they fruit from microscopic spores that cover their bodies. In order to grow, they need to draw nourishment from a material like sawdust, grain, wood chips, or wooden plugs. Spores are blended with a specific amount of the material to create spawn. The spawn acts similarly to the starter used to make sourdough bread. It creates a nurturing environment for the spores to prosper and grow.

Once the spawn starts to grow, sending out thin, white roots called mycelium, then it is time to add it to a growing medium to produce a harvest. Mushrooms can grow straight from the spawn, however, using a growing mediumincreases the yields.

The growing medium, also called a substrate, can be the same as the original material used: sawdust, grain, or wood chips. It can also be a variety of other materials, like logs, coffee grounds, hay, straw, compost, cardboard, rice, corncobs, and banana waste, or a blend of several of those. The choice of substrate varies widely with

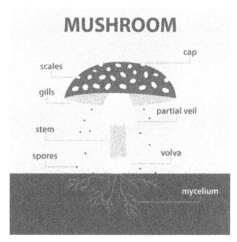

Picture 6: Mushroom Structure. Ardely/Shutterstock.com

mushroom species. Some can grow on many different substrates while others are only able to grow on one type.

15

Once the spawn has been added to the substrate, then it is just a matter of waiting and climate regulation. The amount of time needed to achieve the first flush varies according to mushroom type and can vary from 3 weeks to 2 years. The ideal climate also varies by mushroom type. Before you decide which type to grow, you will need to make sure you have the appropriate substrate available to you and that you can provide the climate needed.

Mushrooms really like cool, dark, humid, and moist growing conditions. A basement is a great growing space. A dark bathroom or space under the sink works well too for many varieties. Generally, they don't need a lot of space. Before deciding where to grow the mushrooms, you will need to investigate the temperature of the space, the temperature needs of the specific strain of mushroom, and how much light the space receives. Mushrooms like Shiitake grow on logs and so need to be outdoors where the climate is less controllable.

CHAPTER 2:

BIOLOGY AND LIFE CYCLE OF THE

MUSHROOM

The more you understand about mushrooms, the more effective your efforts at cultivation will be. So, let's take a look at the biology and life cycle of the mushroom. Warning: unless you're a fan of biology and mycology, you may have to suppress a yawn at the technical jargon that follows. However, it's worth soaking up all the information you can about the mushroom, how it grows, and what's going on at every level of the process. When you're looking at a beautiful, healthy flush, you'll know it's been worth a bit of reading.

ABOUT THE MUSHROOM

First, if you've been paying attention, you know that the mushroom itself is only a part of a larger organism. It is the sex organ, or scientifically the "aerial fruiting body", of an organism that extends below ground in a system of tubular threads called **hyphae**. Collectively, this system of threads is known as a **mycelium**. Essentially, mycelia grow through their food. The hyphae release digestive enzymes at their tips and then absorb the nutrients of the digested substrate as they grow.

Fungi can be saprotrophs, mycorrhizae, or parasites. Saprotrophs grow through and consume decaying matter. Parasitic fungi grow within a host, often killing it in the process. Mycorrhizal fungi have a symbiotic relationship with the roots of plants, and without them, most plants would be unable to grow. In fact, nearly all fungi are benign. In their absence, life on the planet would be impossible.

Fungi are not plants, nor do they have much similarity to plants other than the fact that they are sessile, or fixed in place. They specialize in using the creatures and environmental conditions surrounding them to propagate, and they have developed a number of ingenious techniques to do so. To better understand this, it will be helpful to have a more complete understanding of the structure of the mushroom itself and the part it plays in fungal reproduction.

MUSHROOM STRUCTURE AND FUNGAL SEX

Let's talk about sex. In biological terms, sexual reproduction improves the potential for an organism's survival by allowing them to alter their genetic makeup subtly. These genetic alterations result in physical alterations, some of which have advantages for survival under certain conditions. It's a numbers game, but nature uses this to its advantage. Put enough creatures with different genetic makeups out there, and there is a great likelihood that at least a few of them will have genetic and structural advantages.

Sexual reproduction is accomplished with gametes, cells that have half the normal complement of genetic material. In humans, sperm and egg cells are the gametes. In macrofungi or fungi that produce mushrooms, the gametes are the **spores**. Spores are housed on the **pileus** or underside of the cap. The pileus is often lined with gills which radiate symmetrically from the stem or **stipe**. These gills are lined with basidia, tiny structures shaped like baseball bats. Each basidium contains four horn-like structures called sterigma, and each sterigma holds one spore. The four spores housed on a single basidium are the product of a single event of meiosis, or sexual recombination.

Spores are compact cells surrounded by a protective shielding. They are capable of surviving extremely harsh conditions. Spores will remain dormant until they find appropriate substrates and conditions, at which time they will germinate and begin to grow a primary mycelium. It is known as a primary mycelium because two compatible primary mycelia must find one another and join before they are capable of sexual reproduction. You can think of it as a sperm spore and an egg spore, each producing a mycelium until they encounter a suitable mate. Once they find suitable mates, they unite to form an "adult" mycelium capable, once it grows sufficiently, of producing aerial fruiting bodies.

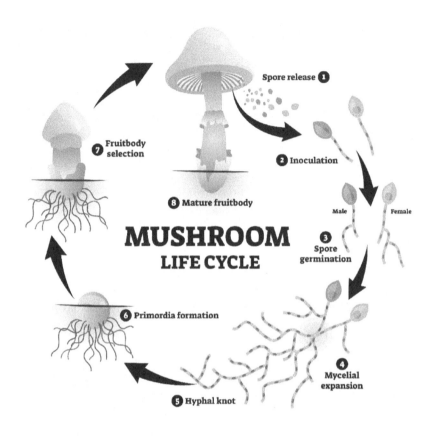

Picture 7: Life Cycle of a Mushroom. Eduards Normaals/Shutterstock.com

One of the coolest things about this is that mushrooms have more "genders", or mating types, than just male and female. In fact, there are thousands, and among these thousands, only certain types will be compatible with any given mating type. Though all of this is happening at a micro level, fungi are as particular about their mates as we are. And, once they unite, they remain in the process of foreplay until the aerial fruiting bodies produce spores. The genetic material of both gametes remains separated in the mycelial cells, each containing two nuclei until the process of meiosis creates spores.

When the "adult" mycelium is formed (in scientific terms, they are called dikaryotic because each cell contains two nuclei with distinct genetic material), it will grow through the medium until triggered by an environmental event. At this point, the hyphae grow into knotted structures termed **primordia**. The primordia are also known as **pins** or **pinheads**, and the process is termed **pinning**. At this point, the hyphal cells begin to differentiate. On a cellular level, they make miniature mushrooms. Individual cells will differentiate into the structure of caps, gills, spores, stipes, etc. Dense white walls called **septa** collect around these structures, effectively dividing them from the surrounding mycelium.

The primordium contains all of the cells which will be present in the fully-grown mushroom. All that remains is for them to absorb sufficient water and expand to full size. This process happens very quickly, which is why mushrooms seem to spring up overnight after a period of rain. As they grow, the primordia take on the characteristic qualities of the mushroom.

The stipe then grows and the spherical cap begins to flatten. As it does so, it stretches the membrane which connects the cap to the stalk and contains the spores within a protective compartment. This membrane is known as a **partial veil** until the gills expand enough to break the veil away from the stipe. When the veil pulls away, it releases the spores and leaves a skirt known as an **annulus** on the stem.

Picture 8: Mushroom Gills. Timothy Dykes/Unsplash.com

Picture 9: Spore Print (Agaricus). Lorenzo Martinelli/Shutterstock.com

In nature, once the veil breaks and exposes the spores which line the gills, the pileus will begin to condense water on the sterigma. Once the water droplets get large enough, they will catapult the droplet and spore out of the gill where air flow can take it away from the fruiting body. At this point, the cycle starts again with a new spore.

Picture 10: Spore Growth on Compost (Button Mushroom).
Rootstock/Shutterstock.com

Picture 11: Mycelium Growing (Button Mushroom).
Dmytro Ostapenko/Shutterstock.com

CHAPTER 3:

BEST MUSHROOMS TO GROW

There are a number of mushroom species that do well in a home-growing environment. It is recommended to choose from this list since the growing methods have been tested many times with success. The easiest mushroom to grow, and the one that most people start with, is the oyster mushroom. Button mushrooms (**Agaricus bisporus)** and Shiitake (**Lentinula edodes)** are also popular choices.

OYSTER MUSHROOMS (*Pleurotus ostreatus*)

- Ideal fruiting temperature: 55-65 °F.
- 4-6 weeks until first flush
- Grows best on straw

The Oyster mushroom is the most popular choice to grow because it can grow on a wide variety of substrates, and when it spawns it is prolific, providing an abundant bounty. Another draw to growing oyster mushrooms is that they are quick to spawn and produce a crop in 4-6 weeks. A crop will usually fruit 3 times before the oyster mushroom mycelium wears out. So, every 7-14 days you will have a new flush of mushrooms. Oyster mushrooms also don't take up a lot of space and can be grown in small or limited areas. For a beginner to the mushroom cultivation world, this is the perfect one to start growing.

The name Oyster is thought to be a reference to the flavor of this mushroom. It doesn't taste exactly like the oyster mollusk; however, it does have a slightly similar familiarity to it. Oyster mushrooms are commonly white, grow in a fan shape with a short stem and have gills running underneath their caps.

Oyster mushrooms can be grown on straw, hay, wood pellets, coffee grounds, sawdust, corn, banana waste matter, paper, and on many hardwood logs.

Another fun reason to grow Oyster mushrooms is because of the color options. The most common variety is a light grayish color. However, they also come in pink, green, and yellow. The pink ones are especially breathtaking to see.

TYPES OF OYSTER MUSHROOMS

Pearl Oyster Mushroom (Pleurotus ostreatus)
One of the most commonly available varieties, the Pearl Oyster mushroom is a light pearl-white color when young and turns darker with age. It is also called the Common Oyster mushroom, Winter

Oyster mushroom, and Grey Oyster mushroom. It grows best in cool temperatures. The Pearl Oyster mushroom smells slightly like almonds and has a dense, meaty texture. It is widely used in culinary applications, as a delicacy in Asia and as a staple meat substitute in Russia and other countries. [Ideal temperature range: 12-18 °C (45-65 °F).]

Picture 12: Pearl Oyster. Berke/Shutterstock.com

Blue Oyster Mushroom

(Pleurotus ostreatus var. columbinus)

A sub-species of the Pearl Oyster mushroom, the Blue Oyster is stunning with its contrasting blue-grey caps and light blue gills. This strain also prefers cool growing temperatures. The taste and texture of the Blue Oyster mushroom is the same as the Pearl Oyster. The only significant difference is the color. [Ideal temperature range: 12-18 °C (45-65 °F).]

Picture 13: Blue Oyster. Orlio/Shutterstock

Phoenix Oyster Mushroom (Pleurotus pulmonarius)

The Phoenix Oyster mushroom prefers warmer temperatures in contrast to the Pearl and Blue varieties. Depending on the strain, it can be a brownish-tan color or white. The Phoenix Oyster mushroom is also known as the Indian Oyster mushroom, Italian Oyster mushroom, Lung Oyster mushroom, and Summer Oyster mushroom. This variety also tastes similar to the Pearl Oyster. [Ideal temperature range: 18-30 °C (64-86 °F).]

Picture 14: Phoenix Oyster. Xiebiyun/Shutterstock.com

Golden Oyster Mushroom (Pleurotus citrinopileatus)

Another warmer temperature Oyster mushroom, the Golden Oyster mushroom gets its name from its striking yellow color. It is also called the Yellow Oyster mushroom. This variety has a thinner, more delicate, flesh than other varieties and is quite fragrant. [Ideal temperature range: 18-30 °C (64-86 °F).]

Picture 15: Golden Oyster. Irina Anatoleva/Shutterstock.com

*Pink Oyster Mushroom (*Pleurotus djamor)

The vivid pink of the Pink Oyster mushroom along with its unique ruffled edges make it a popular strain to grow. It is also referred to as the Flamingo Oyster mushroom, Salmon Oyster mushroom, and Strawberry Oyster mushroom. Unfortunately, the brilliant pink fades when the mushroom is cooked. It has a stronger flavor than other oyster varieties and is a bit tougher as well. It prefers warm temperatures. [Ideal temperature range: 18-30 °C (64-86 °F).]

Picture 16: Pink Oyster. Cora Mueller/Shutterstock.com

*King Oyster Mushroom (*Pleurotus eryngii*)*

The King Oyster mushroom is truly royalty when it comes to cooking. Of all the Oyster varieties, it most emulates meat in texture and flavor. It is much larger than the other Oyster mushrooms and is also more difficult to grow. It is not the easiest for beginners. King Oyster mushrooms like cool temperatures. [Ideal temperature range: 12-18 °C (45-65 °F).]

Picture 17: King Oyster.
Jiang Hongyan/Shutterstock.com

SHIITAKE (*Lentinula edodes*)

- Ideal Fruiting Temperature: 50-70 °F
- 3 months until first flush
- Grows best on logs

The shiitake mushroom is regarded all over the world for its culinary and medicinal uses. They are native to East Asia but are widely grown and can be found in markets across the world. Shiitakes are meaty and firm in texture and have an earthy fragrance and flavor. When they are dried, they become smoky and rich. Shiitakes make excellent dried jerky.

Shiitake mushrooms are the second most common mushroom grown in the world. They are easy to grow and produce abundantly. They look like a classic mushroom with a rounded fleshy top that is a shade of brown. They are short and stout, growing around 2-4 inches in diameter. Underneath the caps are white gills and a short stem.

Unlike the majority of other mushrooms, shiitakes prefer being grown on hardwood logs, like oak, maple, ironwood, and beech via plugs. Plugs are mycelium-infused dowels that get tapped into the logs. Shiitakes are not a great choice if you have limited space to grow. Inoculated logs can produce flushes in as little as six months and can go on for several years. This mushroom takes longer to set up for growing than many others, however, the multiple year harvests make it entirely worthwhile.

Picture 18: Shiitake. Phloen Khamkaeo/Shutterstock.com

The strains of Shiitake mushroom plugs which are available on the market vary widely. There are no standard varieties like there are with the Oyster mushrooms. Most fungi spawn sellers will just call it Shiitake and there is only one choice, or they will have several strains that are specific to their company. There are types that do better in different weather climates so be sure to pick one that works for your location.

BUTTON MUSHROOMS (*Agaricus bisporus*)

- Ideal fruiting temperature: 60-74 °F
- 6-8 weeks to first flush
- Grows best on manure blend

Picture 19: Button. Robert Latawiec/Shutterstock.com

The most popular mushroom in the world, this little mushroom is the one you usually see in every grocery store. Don't pass them by because of their commonality, though. Button mushrooms are really easy to grow and they grow abundantly. Once you've experienced the bounties of growing Button mushrooms, you'll be hooked! They can fruit several times from one spore, so you will have multiple harvests from one container.

Button mushrooms can be grown outdoors or indoors so you can plan to have them all year round, regardless of the season. That is awesome!

A fun Button mushroom fact: Portobello and Cremini mushrooms are actually types of Button mushrooms. Creminis are a brown-capped version of the Button and Portobellos are Cremini mushrooms that have been allowed to grow large.

Picture 20: Cremini. Svetlana Lukienko/Shutterstock.com

Picture 21: Portobello. spicyPXL/Shutterstock.com

ENOKITAKE (*Flammulina velutipes*)

- Idea fruiting temperature: 40-50 °F
- 6-8 weeks until first flush
- Grows best on supplemented hardwood

Also commonly called Enoki, these mushrooms are wildly unique and fun to grow. The wild and cultivated versions of Enokitake are vastly different. The cultivated version doesn't get the same access to sunlight and so it grows in tall, white, leggy, stalks that clump together and look like a bunch of bean sprouts gathered together. They are used frequently in soups and a have a crisp, radish-like flavor.

Picture 22: Enokitake. Pholawat Khorjanklang/Shutterstock.com

Enokitake mushrooms are a winter-fruiting mushroom and can be grown on a variety of substrates. They like the cold so much they can even grow in the refrigerator. The common practice to keep their stems so long and leggy is to grow them in jars or cylinders. They will fruit anywhere from a few weeks to a few months. After the first fruiting, they will produce several more harvests over a period of 6-8 weeks.

The size and shape of Enokitake you grow will depend on temperatures, growing substrate, and environment.

LION'S MANE *(Hericium erinaceus)*

- Ideal fruiting temperature: 60-70 °F
- 8-10 weeks until first flush
- Grows best on supplemented hardwood

Picture 23: Lion's Mane. Mimpuy/Shutterstock.com

Another spectacular-looking mushroom, Lion's Mane is one that you will never mistake for anything else. In the wild, it grows on the side of trees and looks like a large ball of white shaggy icicles, or a giant shaggy cheerleader's pom-pom. This type is also commonly referred to as Bearded Tooth. The species are referred to as comb-tooth mushrooms, probably because they look like they need a good combing!

Lion's Mane bruises easily when handled so it isn't often found in grocery stores. This makes it an excellent variety for home-growers since it is likely that is the only way you will be able to have it. These mushrooms grow quickly once they fruit and you can go from a small, marble-size fruit to a softball size or larger in less than a week. The big downside, though, is that to get the Lion's Mane to fruit initially can involve a long wait, sometimes up to a year.

Besides its appearance, Lion's Mane also stands out in flavor. It is oddly similar in texture to crab meat and other seafood. When it is sautéed with butter, it brings out a seafood-like flavor as well. This mushroom is used a lot as a meat substitute in cooking.

Lion's Mane is actually a broad name used for several types that are related yet are slightly different in appearance. They all have the bright white color and shag formation, however there are varieties in the types of shag and hence the different names. The different types all taste similar; most people don't notice much of a difference in flavor at all.

TYPES OF LION'S MANE MUSHROOMS

Bear's Head Tooth (Hericium americanum)

This variety has downward-pointing, medium length white teeth, or icicles, hanging in grouped bundles from its center mass. The main way to tell the difference between Lion's Mane and Bear's Head is that the Lion's Mane is a singular, rounded ball, while the Bear's Head looks like a crowd of shaggy clumps gathered together.

Picture 24: Bear's Head Tooth. Cor van der Waal/Shutterstock.com

Comb Tooth (H. coralloides)

The Comb Tooth has crowded shaggy clumps like the Bear's Head, however, it differs in that the ends of the clumps are shorter and the ends are more ornamental. Whenever I see a Comb Tooth, I am reminded of paper snowflake cut-outs with their jagged edges and intricate designs.

The spores of the Lion's Mane, or Hericium erinaceus, are often the only spores you can find online. There is a market developing, however, for the other varieties, and a quick internet search can reveal a few sources of the others as well.

Picture 25: Comb Tooth.
Henri Koskinen/Shutterstock.com

39

WINE CAP *(Stropharia rugoso annulata)*

- Ideal fruiting temperature: 55-50 °F
- 6 months to 1 year until first flush
- Grows best in mulch

The Wine Cap mushroom is truly something to behold. If allowed to grow to their full size, they are 12+ inches in diameter and weigh 3-4 pounds. That's a big mushroom! It has a burgundy red cap (hence its name), grey gills and a thick, stout, white stalk. The texture is firm yet tender and they taste slightly earthy and nutty. Some have described their flavor as a combination of potatoes and red wine.

Wine Cap mushrooms are almost unbelievably easy to grow. A little garden is all that is needed to set them up outside and once established, Wine Cap spawn will happily fruit out there year after year. Be ready for hundreds of pounds of mushrooms! If you want to grow them indoors, they are amenable to that as well. Their fruiting time won't last as long in indoor situations, yet it will still be quite bountiful.

This mushroom grows best in a bed of wood chips in partial sunlight. It is one of the only mushrooms that prefers some sun. If you start them outside in the spring, you can have a crop in several months.

MAITAKE *(grifola frondosa)*

- Ideal fruiting temperature: 55-65 °F
- 4-6 months to first flush
- Grows best on supplemented hardwood

Picture 26: Maitake. Jreika/Shutterstock

Maitake, the love of chefs the world over, takes a bit more effort and experience than the other mushrooms in this list. It is entirely worth it, I promise. Also known as Hen of the Woods, this mushroom grows in large clumps with multiple fronds that resemble the feathers of a hen. It can grow up to 50 lbs. in weight in the right circumstances, however, 10-15 pounds is more normal. That is still a massive mushroom! The texture is dense and meaty and it tastes mild and earthy. Its simple flavor and excellent texture make it the perfect substitute for, or complement to meats, which is why chefs treasure it. It is truly a versatile mushroom that goes with almost anything.

The difficult part of growing Maitake is the stages it needs to develop correctly and the need for patience. It needs a specific temperature and environment to fruit and will need to be watered daily if indoors. Indoor cultivation will take 3-4 months to fruit. If they are set up outdoors, it can take a year or maybe longer. They are slow growers. Once they take hold, however, they will fruit for many years afterwards. Outdoor cultivation requires inoculating logs.

QUICK LOOK: Harvesting Times

	Avg. Harvest Indoor	Avg. Harvest Outdoor	Avg. Number of Flushes	Taste
Oyster Mushrooms	4-6 weeks	6mo-1 year	3 indoors, 3 years outdoors	mild, sweet, earthy, meaty
Enokitake Mushrooms	6-8 weeks	6mo-1 year	3 indoors, 3 years outdoors	crunchy, mild, fresh
Shiitake Mushrooms	3 months	1 -2 years	2 indoors, 4 years outdoors	earthy, smoky, meaty
Lion's Mane Mushroom	8-10 weeks	1-2 years	2 indoors, 2 years outdoors	sweet, savory, crab-like texture
Wine Cap Mushrooms	N/a	6mo – 1 year	3 years outdoors	mild, nutty
Maitake	3-4 months	1-2 years	1 indoors, 3 years outdoors	firm, woods, earthy

CHOOSING WHICH MUSHROOM TO GROW

This is where the tough decisions happen! If you're at all like me, they all sound amazing and you want to get started growing all of them. Of course, it's best to start with just one or two and see how it goes. Then, if you like it, add some more and pretty soon you are the envy of all your neighbors as you enjoy your bounty.

Seriously, though, there are several factors that need to be thought through when deciding which will work best for the space you have available for growing. The main considerations are indoors vs. outdoors, time, and space.

INDOORS VS. OUTDOORS

All the mushrooms listed can be grown indoors or outdoors, depending on your climate. Growing mushrooms indoors decreases the time it takes for them to fruit, since their environment is controlled for optimal conditions. Mushrooms grown indoors have a shorter lifespan, though. They often fruit 2-3 times over the space of several weeks to a month and then the mycelium is expended. If you want to grow more, you will need to purchase more spawn or spores.

Mushrooms grown outdoors take a lot longer to fruit than those grown indoors. Sometimes the difference is quite significant, up to a year longer. The bonus, however, is that once the mycelium takes hold, it will produce for several years and you will have an annual crop of mushrooms with minimal effort. Nice!

The climate where you live will, of course, have an effect on your mushroom-growing adventures if you choose to grow outdoors. Climates with high humidity are great for the final fruiting stage of many mushrooms; however, it also can't be too hot. Some varieties of mushrooms need a cold "season" shock in order to start growing. Living in a place where there are noticeable seasonal temperature changes, like autumn and winter, will help your outdoor success for most of the species mentioned here.

Oysters, Buttons, Enokitake, Lion's Mane, and Maitake are best grown indoors. Wine Cap and Shiitake are best grown outdoors. Wine Cap mushrooms are the only ones that do not thrive at all inside, even though it can be done. In the next chapters, we will go into detail about how to grow each one of these in their ideal condition.

TIME

In general, growing mushrooms isn't largely time-consuming like vegetable or flower gardening. The set-up is generally easy with just a few steps and then it is a matter of monitoring temperature, humidity, and watching the mycelium grow. The fun, or maybe frustrating, part of growing mushrooms is that there is rarely such a thing as an immediate result. Fungi take their time to grow and spread. They can be fickle and wait until they have the perfect environment.

If you want to see quicker results, choose an indoor mushroom. Oysters, Buttons, and Enokitake are the fastest indoor growers, producing a harvest in as little as 4 weeks for some strains. For most though, it can be closer to 2-3 months or longer. Lion's Mane and Maitake take about 3 months to incubate and fruit when grown indoors.

Shiitake and Wine Caps grown outdoors, take 4 months to a year to fruit. Mushrooms can be hard to predict though. There are a lot of variables and it has been known to happen that just as you think the mycelium hasn't taken hold, all of a sudden you have bunches of mushrooms. Or, you need to start over and try again. This can be especially frustrating if you've already been waiting patiently for a year or more to see it happen.

SPACE

Growing mushrooms indoors doesn't take a lot of space unless you are intending to start a mushroom farm. A bag or block of substrate doesn't take up a lot of room and since most mushrooms thrive in dark or mostly dark, cool areas, they can be tucked in places that otherwise aren't being used, like under counters or in the basement.

Wine Caps being grown outdoors don't need a lot of room either. The more room you provide, the more mushrooms will grow, but they don't need a lot to get started.

For the mushrooms that grow on logs, like Shiitake, Oyster, and Maitake, the amount of outdoor space you will need will depend entirely on how much you plan to grow. One log doesn't take up much room. Stacks of logs will require more space, of course.

CLIMATE

All the mushrooms listed grow in the wild in places with seasonal temperature changes, like the Pacific Northwest of the United States. It's okay if you don't live in an ideal temperature, though. In your backyard, you can create a micro-climate to benefit the mycelium's growth. If you live in a location where you cannot manage the variables outside then it is best to choose an indoor growing method.

A micro-climate is the climate of a very specific place, for example the spot in your backyard. The micro-climate often differs from the climate of the surrounding area. To create a micro-climate for your outdoor mushrooms, there are two main variables you need to consider. The first is humidity. Mushrooms need humidity. The mushroom patch should have easy and ready access to water. Installing a shade cloth over the mushrooms will help too, as well as keeping out pests. The second factor is temperature. Each mushroom type has a different need when it comes to ideal fruiting temperature. This can be hard to regulate outside. Shaded locations are best for keeping temperatures down. If you can keep some type of control over the temperature and humidity, you are bound to have success.

CHAPTER 4:

AN OVERVIEW OF THE CULTIVATION PROCESS

Whenever we cultivate an organism, we duplicate, in a controlled setting, all the conditions necessary for propagation and growth. So, having heard and understood all aspects of the mushroom life cycle in nature, you will find it easier to understand the process of cultivation and the steps we take along the way.

Nature plays a numbers game, creating so many spores that one or a few are bound to work out. However, when cultivating, we are able to create conditions which favor growth. The skilled cultivator can select the best specimens from one flush to use in later inoculations, refining the species one generation at a time.

Let's look at the basic stages of cultivation. This will help you to understand how to navigate these stages and apply them to your own cultivation process.

STAGES OF CULTIVATION

Cultivation goes through a process of three stages: **germination**, **expansion**, and **fruiting**. Germination is the process where the spore finds suitable conditions and begins to grow a primary mycelium. Once compatible strains meet and mate, they enter the process of expansion. The adult (dikaryotic) mycelium then grows through the medium. Finally, the adult mycelium will fruit.

One thing that's really cool to understand is that mushrooms are essentially immortal.

When you move on to the expansion stage, you transfer the culture which you have identified onto a suitable substrate. In many cases, this substrate is sterilized whole grain in quart- or pint-sized Mason jars. If you are buying your spawn from a retailer, this is the process they are using to create volumes of spawn. The purpose of the expansion phase is to give the mycelium time and space to grow to a volume sufficient for proper fruiting. The spawn can be introduced to the grain and spread through it, creating a fungal spawn run. In this stage, you'll often need to shake the grain every few days to create space in the mixture and allow the mycelium to colonize it more effectively. The spawn can be transferred to larger Mason jars or plastic bags to expand the mycelial mass.

Once you have generated sufficient spawn, it can be transferred to a final fruiting substrate, the medium used to promote growth of the mushrooms or fruiting bodies. The fruiting substrate will depend upon the mushroom strain. Wood-loving species will fruit only on beds of wood chips or other substrates with high lignin content.

You'll likely want to cover the fruiting substrate with a protective layer like peat moss or dry vermiculite. In addition, temperature, air exchange, light, and humidity must all be within the appropriate range to promote fruiting.

THE THREE STAGES OF BASIC HOME GROWING

1. Acquire Mushroom Spawn
2. Inoculate Substrate
3. Monitor Humidity, Temperature, and Light until mushrooms fruit

The spawn needed to inoculate your fruiting substrate will have to be acquired. There are a large number of retailers online who offer a big variety of mushrooms, types, strains, and species. Read all the information before you buy since some spawn are best for specific temperatures and substrates.

After you receive the mushroom spawn of choice, you will need to inoculate the substrate. In another chapter further along, I outline 7 of the most popular inoculation methods. There are a lot to choose from!

Once your substrate is inoculated, we begin the waiting game. During this time, you will need to check on humidity, moisture, light, and temperature on a frequent basis to make sure conditions are right for your growing mushrooms.

DIY VS. READY-MADE CULTIVATION KITS

There are a variety of ready-made kits that you can find online. If you are a first-time cultivator or you plan to cultivate only a single batch, these kits may be the best way to go. They can also be suitable if you want to obtain a particular strain for spore syringes. Ready-made kits take most of the headache out of growing, as they have been prepared under sterile conditions and require no more than a bit of light, water, and attention. However, if you want to take your cultivation journey beyond a few flushes, then you'll want to go the extra mile.

Ready-made kits are great for first-time growers to see if mushroom growing is really what they are interested in. It gives a good feel for what is involved in growing mushrooms. Additionally, most of these kits are guaranteed in some way to produce, which is a nice benefit.

Buying spores or spawn and preparing and inoculating your own substrate takes much more time, of course. However, it also allows you a lot more variability in type and method. It is also significantly less expensive to do it yourself.

CHAPTER 5:

OPTIMAL MUSHROOM GROWING

CONDITIONS

Each variety and fungus strain will have its own growing conditions and requirements. In this chapter, I will go over the commonalities and then go into detail about what each variety needs. Mushrooms grow differently than plants and vegetables and so a lot of this may sound new and unusual. Take the time to understand each mushroom's needs and it will take you far in achieving a successful mushroom crop!

LIGHT

Unlike the majority of plants, mushrooms do not get the majority of their nutrients from the sun. They do not need a lot of light. This does not mean they need total darkness, though. Many do well with some light, it just isn't necessary. One benefit to growing them in darker spaces is that it preserves moisture, which is a necessity for mushrooms to reproduce and release their spores. Basements are a popular option for ideal darkness and moistness. Underneath kitchen sinks, tucked away in closets, and a variety of other spaces have been utilized by mushroom growers.

Mushrooms like Buttons are best grown in a dark, cool, indoor space. A basement is pretty perfect for them. Oysters, Shiitake, Enokitake, Lion's Mane, and Maitake all want a bit of light during their fruiting stage to develop large, lush caps. Wine Cap mushrooms do great in partial shade.

MOISTURE

In order to thrive, mushrooms need a moist environment. The growing substrate should not dry out easily and should hold a good amount of moisture. Some mushrooms, like Shiitake on logs, will need to be soaked in drums of water during dry spells to maintain an appropriate moisture content. An average moisture content for mushrooms is for them to be kept moist but not soaking wet or soggy.

HUMIDITY

Moisture and humidity are not the same thing. Humidity is a measured percentage of the moisture in the air, regardless of temperature. Basically, moisture is the water in liquid state and humidity is the water in vapor state. Warm air holds more moisture than cold air. Mushrooms like lots of moisture in the air when they are growing. This means maintaining a warm space where the water can stay in the air.

TEMPERATURE

The temperatures that mushrooms require generally fall within 10-25 °C/50 – 80 °F. The colonization process, when the mycelium spreads over the substrate like roots, can handle a wider range of temperatures. It is a more forgiving time because you are only asking the mycelium to spread out, not produce mushrooms yet. Usually, this can be done at room temperature. The fruiting temperature, when the mushroom actually begins to form pins, is much more specific and specialized for each type. For optimal results, double check the specific needs for the mushroom you are growing. This can also vary by strain; for example, there are Shiitake spawn that are developed for specific climates and are described based on ideal fruiting temperature. It may be necessary to have heaters or fans installed in your growing area to maintain the correct temperature indoors.

NUTRIENTS/SUBSTRATE

Mushrooms take the nutrients they need to grow from the organic material (substrate) they are growing in. The specific nutrients they need are protein, nitrogen, fats, starch, and lignin. Which organic material works best varies by mushroom variety. Button mushrooms thrive on prepared compost substrates, while Shiitake mushrooms can get all the nutrients they need from logs or sawdust.

QUICK LOOK: Optimal Growing Conditions

Mush-room Variety	Coloniz ation Tempe rature	Fruit-ing Tempe rature	Light	Moistu re	Hum idity	Prefer-red Substrat es
Oyster	15-20 °C/60-70 °F	12-23 °C/55-75 °F	Indire ct	Average	High	All
Button	21-23 °C/70-75 °F	13-16 °C/57-62 °F	None	Medium	High	Prepared Compost
Shiitake	15-23 °C/60-75 °F	10-21 °C/50-70 °F	Indire ct/Sha de	Average	High	Logs, Sawdust logs
Enoki-take	15-23 °C/60-75 °F	4-10 °C/40-50 °F	Indire ct	Average	High	Sawdust logs, Bottles, Mulch
Lion's Mane	15-20 °C/60-70 °F	18-23 °C/65-75 °F	Indire ct	High	High	Sawdust logs, Outdoor logs
Wine Caps	20-26 °C/70-80 °F	10-12 °C/50-55 °F	Sun/ Partial Shade	Medium	Medi um	Lasagna mulch
Maitake	15-23 °C/60-70 °F	12-18 °C/55-65 °F	Indire ct	Light	High	Sawdust logs, Outdoor logs, Bottles

THE BEST PLACE TO GROW MUSHROOMS?

Where to grow, that is the question! With mushrooms, there are so many options it can be entirely overwhelming. There is no right or wrong or better or worse when it comes to deciding whether to grow mushrooms outdoors or indoors. Much will depend on the type of mushroom you want to grow, how fast you want to see results, and resources available to you.

The main reason growers choose indoor cultivation is because it is quicker. And, usually quicker by quite a bit. An Oyster mushroom grown indoors on a sawdust log will produce in a couple months. Oyster mushrooms grown outdoors on logs can take 1-2 years to fruit. Shiitake are similar. Indoors, they fruit within 3-6 months. Outdoors, they can take upwards to 2 years. The same goes with Lion's Mane and Maitake. Button mushrooms are best grown indoors because they crave that dark, damp, space, like the basement.

Of course, choosing to grow mushrooms indoors means you must have the space, and that you are able to provide optimal growing conditions for them. Most don't take up much room at all. One or two grow bags can be tucked away somewhere easily enough. A 5-gallon bucket is easily moved around as needed. A row of Mason jars near a window is easy enough to take care of.

Indoor growing also depends on how many mushrooms you intend to cultivate. Starting small is always best, to make sure it is something you enjoy doing. However, if you're thinking about growing a lot, the indoor space you have available may not be sufficient.

Growing mushrooms indoors requires that you are able to maintain appropriate temperatures, humidity, moisture, and light for them. This can get complicated. You will want equipment like thermometers, humidity sensors, and the like. Also, if you need to purchase straw, nutrients, hardwood sawdust, and mushroom grow bags, it can start adding up monetarily quite a bit.

Indoor growing is also more labor-intensive, in that you will get 2-3 flushes out of one cultivation and then you need to start over again. The harvest is quicker and abundant but they won't reproduce year after year without some effort.

Outdoor growing is great and some people say they can taste the difference between indoor cultivated mushrooms and outdoor cultivated ones. Outdoor growing, as mentioned before, takes much, much, longer. If you have a long-term plan and live on property you own, this is a good choice. It is a way of utilizing your outdoor space in new ways. The biggest benefit of outdoor space is that there is a lot more of it. Instead of growing 5-6 bags of Shiitake in your basement, you could grow them on stacks and stacks of logs outside. Or, you could do both.

Outdoor growing tends to be less expensive as well. There are no multiples of grow bags and supplies needed on a regular basis. If you are inoculating logs from your own land, then you don't even have to worry about buying the substrate. The land will provide it.

The biggest benefit of outdoor growing is the returning yield, year after year. Once the labor is put in to inoculate the mushrooms the first time, it is then just a waiting game each year for them to fruit. You don't have to re-inoculate or buy more materials; Mother Nature takes care of everything. If you intend to grow on logs, they should be cut in the winter or spring for a spring inoculation.

CHAPTER 6:

UNDERSTANDING THE GROWING

PROCESS

All cultivation processes, whether they are indoors or outdoors, regardless of the method of cultivation used, follow the same steps in cultivation. We begin with spores or mycelial cultures. Next, we inoculate a substrate with these cultures, allowing them to colonize to create primary spawn. The primary spawn is intended to let the mycelium take hold. Often, it is then used as an inoculum to generate secondary spawn, a hardier substrate which can be expanded as far as required prior to fruiting.

The next step in the cultivation process is to place a secondary spawn in conditions that promote fruiting. If indoors, we place it in lower temperature conditions with appropriate light. Often, this will require a growing chamber as well. If the mushrooms are outdoors, they will fruit on their logs or mulch when the conditions are right. Next, fruiting substrates will begin to produce flushes, or mushroom harvests. These are then harvested, most often before the cap detaches from the stipe. A single batch will often produce three to five flushes until it must be retired, unless it becomes contaminated prior to this.

After the mushrooms are harvested, they are processed. Often, this means cleaning them up and adding them straight into the frying pan! They can be cooked, dried, frozen, and so much more. Sometimes, they will be brewed into a tea. Alcohol infusions will work as well. Dried mushrooms and alcohol infusions can be stored for months, however, a mushroom tea will only last for about a month, and even then, only if it is refrigerated.

Finally, we come full circle back to the beginning. Harvested mushrooms can be used to create spore prints or spore syringes for later inoculations. Alternately, the mycelium from the stem of a prized specimen can be used to clone mycelial cultures.

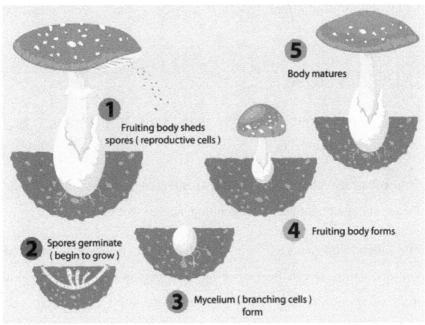

Eknarin Maphichai/Shutterstock.com

The method of cultivation will have an impact on the steps of the process. For example, wood-loving mushrooms often use a sheet of cardboard to cover the secondary substrate during colonization. The cardboard often becomes inoculated with mycelium and can then be used to inoculate primary substrate. This can also be done by placing stems of wood-loving mushrooms between layers of cardboard and purposely colonizing them for later inoculations.

Let's take a detailed look at all the steps in the process:

PREPARATION

The first step is to obtain spawn. It is possible to do this at home; however, the process is tricky. For first-time or new growers, it is recommended to purchase already-prepared spawn. There are many online companies that sell a wide variety of species and options.

INOCULATION

Once you have your spawn, the next step is to introduce it to a prepared substrate.

The substrate must be carefully protected from contamination. Please see the chapters about keeping a clean work space.

The inoculation process varies depending on the growing method you are using. It can be rather quick if you are just doing a few indoor bags or sawdust logs. If you are inoculating logs outdoors or making a mulch bed, it can be quite a bit more time-consuming.

COLONIZATION

After your primary substrate has been inoculated, you will want to store it in a dark place with the temperature between 75 and 85°

Fahrenheit. You will see the colonies begin to form within the substrate as networks of white fibers.

Full colonization will usually occur within 1-2 weeks. In essence, you have created mycelial spawn at this point. When the mycelium completely covers the grains in the jar, you can either proceed to the fruiting stage or use this as spawn to inoculate further substrate.

EXPANDING SPAWN

If you wish to expand your spawn before moving into the fruiting stage, you can mix the colonized grain with further substrate. This is often done using spawn bags. After filling the bags with a whole grain/vermiculite mix, blend 1-2 cups with each bag. Seal the bags with an impulse sealer, and then repeat the incubation process.

You can do this as many times as you like until you have the desired amount of substrate. At this point, it is considered secondary substrate. The fully-colonized grain serves as a primary substrate with a well-established mycelium. You can mix hydrogen peroxide with all spawn bags in the same ratio as described above (About 80ml per spawn bag. Make sure the substrate is as dry as possible).

If you are using a wood-loving mushroom, you can mix the primary substrate with a blend of wood chips and sawdust without sterilization. Wood-loving mushrooms are far more resistant to contamination than other species. The spawn should be stored at temperatures between 75 and 85 °Fahrenheit while incubating.

PREPARING THE GROW CHAMBER

Depending on your growing method, the grow chamber is either filled with secondary substrate or lined with perlite. The inoculated cakes are placed on this layer directly from the jars, without being broken apart. These growing chambers must be kept in sterile conditions to prevent contamination. If they are misted regularly and provided about 8 hours of light per day, they will begin to pin within a couple of weeks. Pinning is the process of creating primordia, or immature mushrooms. After this occurs, you should have your first flush within a week.

Alternately, the fruiting substrate can be spread across the bottom of a sterilized growing chamber. You will want to cover the substrate with a layer of casing material to protect it from contaminants and mist it regularly to maintain moisture levels. Pinning and fruiting will occur within the same timeframe, but it will be spread evenly across the growing chamber instead of collected around cakes.

These methods are suitable for indoor growth. It is extremely difficult to get wood-loving mushrooms to fruit indoors.

FRUITING

Fruiting occurs when the primordia mature into full mushrooms. How long this takes will depend on the type of mushroom and what you are growing it on.

While you are tending your colony prior to fruiting, you will want to mist it regularly to keep the moisture levels up. Be careful not to overwater, though, as this can result in mold. Including water crystals in your casing material will reduce the likelihood of it drying out or becoming too wet.

HARVESTING

You will want to harvest your mushrooms right before the veil breaks away from the stem. If you allow the veil to break, the spores will be released, and this can be a bit messy. The only exception to this is if you choose to make spore prints. If so, then you will want to allow the mushroom to spread flat before harvesting it. Remember to choose the best specimens to create spore prints, as you will want to pass those genes on to the next generation.

When harvesting your mushrooms, you will want to grasp the stalk and pull as much as possible out of the casing material and substrate. If you leave a portion of the stem above the casing material, it will be prone to contamination. Often, this will leave a hole in the casing material. You will want to fill this hole with casing material to protect the substrate beneath. If you disturb other small mushrooms when harvesting a mature one, remove them as well. Don't worry about the small loss of material, as the fungus will just redistribute the energy to other mushrooms.

After each flush, your colony will need more water to make up for what is lost. It is better to mist it lightly and frequently rather than to add too much water at once. If at any point you see contamination, don't try to save the colony. Get rid of it before it infects your other growing chambers. Mold spores can spread quickly throughout your entire growing space and contaminate it for days.

One final thing: often there will be pieces of material stuck to the base of the stem when you harvest the mushroom. It's much easier to remove these while the mushroom is fresh. You can simply scrape a knife downward against the bottom of the stipe to remove all excess vermiculite.

GET STARTED GROWING

Are you ready to start your own mushrooms? I hope you are. There is a lot to learn when deciding which growing medium to use and which mushroom you should grow. Really, it all depends on what your goals are. In this section, I will detail the 7 most popular growing methods. I am sure there is one you will like!

TYPES OF SUBSTRATES AND TREATMENTS

A substrate is the bulk material used to grow mushrooms. It provides nutrients and energy to the fruiting mycelium, much like dirt provides nutrients for vegetables. The type of substrate to use depends entirely on what type of mushrooms you are growing. Each mushroom has a preferred substrate and growing method. The Oyster mushroom can be grown in a variety of substrates, while Button mushrooms need a very specific type. When you are deciding which type of mushroom to grow, make sure you understand which substrate to use and that you have the space and resources available to implement it. Please refer to the table in the Optimal Growing Conditions section to see which ones can be used with which mushrooms.

The main types of substrates are:

1. Straw – this must be pasteurized before use to prevent other organisms from taking hold
2. Coffee grounds – inexpensive and easy, albeit limited
3. Hardwood sawdust– a versatile choice which many mushrooms like, needs to be sterilized

4. Compost or Manure blend – for Button mushrooms
5. Coco Coir and Vermiculite – mixed together, they make a great substrate
6. Mulch bed "lasagna" - specifically for Wine Caps
7. Logs – the ideal choice for Shiitake and Maitake

PASTEURIZATION VS. STERILIZATION

Before we get into how to prepare the substrates, I think it's important to understand why the substrate is pasteurized or sterilized before use. This is not a step that should ever be skipped. You will understand why in a moment. The pasteurization or sterilization makes the preparation a lot longer and can be a deterrent for some people wanting to learn how to grow mushrooms because it sounds intimidating. Don't be discouraged! The processes may sound complicated but really, they are not. And once you have done it once or twice, it'll be easy.

The reason the substrates need to be treated is that they are a nutrient source that many species would enjoy. Mold, bacteria, and other mycelium would all happily take up residence if they could. Mold and bacteria grow faster than mycelium and will soak up all the rich nutrients before the mushroom has a chance. Growing mushrooms with an untreated substrate is a sure recipe for failure. In fact, it's likely that whatever substrate you are using already has a bunch of unwelcome visitors in the process of setting up residence. Anything that sits outside for any period of time is susceptible.

Pasteurization and sterilization are not the same things. Pasteurization heats up the substrate to a temperature between 65-80 °C/150-180 °F for 2 hours. Not all the contaminants are removed during this process; however, it gets rid of enough of them that the mushroom has a chance. There are good microorganisms out there that are actually beneficial to the growth of the mushrooms.

Sterilization is a method used to eliminate all, or nearly all, contamination. This is accomplished by heating the substrate under pressure for a period of time. This technique requires a pressure cooker. The temperature needs to go up to 120 °C/250 °F in order to kill off everything.

Different substrates need different processing. Supplemented sawdust substrates need full sterilization because they are nutrient-rich and therefore at a higher risk of contamination. Straw and non-supplemented sawdust only need pasteurization because they have less nutrients, therefore making them less attractive to contaminants. Coffee grounds, cardboard, compost, Coco coir, and vermiculite require pasteurization as well and not just sterilization. The compost, if you are buying it, should already be pasteurized.

KEEPING A STERILE ENVIRONMENT

Since we just talked about sterilization and pasteurization, it is a good time to talk about how and why it is important to keep a sterile environment as well. This is mainly important during the inoculation phase. It's quite impossible to keep a totally sterile environment but we can increase the odds of our mushrooms fruiting if we get close.

As mentioned before, there are bacteria, molds, and other microbes in the air and all around looking for a nice place to inhabit. The substrate is sterilized or pasteurized before use, however that is not where the concern ends. As soon as the material is removed from the sterilization or pasteurization process and is exposed to air, it is at risk all over again. This is one of the most crucial times in your cultivation process. The substrate has had most other organisms removed from it and now the challenge is to get the mushroom spawn to it before any other organisms make a dash for it. Not to sound melodramatic, but it is heart-breaking when all your hard work goes to waste because of one small mold spore.

If you open the bag or jar of treated substrate and leave it open for even the smallest amount of time, microorganisms in the air can take full advantage. And they will. Never ever open the bag until you are ready to inoculate. And never leave it open longer than necessary. In the case of log-growing, the time that you drill the hole is the sensitive time and it is important to push the plugs or sawdust into the holes as soon as possible. Also, sealing the plugged hole with wax is a great way to keep out contaminants.

It may sound odd that mushrooms need such a sterile environment; after all, they grow in all kinds of conditions in the wild. Wild mushrooms are built to deal with a large variety of temperatures and contaminants. And, if they don't like the conditions, they don't grow. It happens all the time (says the frustrated wild mushroom forager!). When we propagate mushrooms and isolate mycelium strands, we are changing the mushroom's natural process and therefore we need to create an artificial environment to help it grow.

FIGHTING AIRBORNE CONTAMINANTS

The first type of contaminants to fight against are airborne ones. They are everywhere and we can't see them. Just wonderful! To keep them at bay, a Laminar Flow Hood is ideal. The flow hoods provide a clean stream of air that keeps airborne contaminants away while you are working with your treated substrate and spawn. Unfortunately, these are very expensive. They are way outside the budget for the hobby mushroom grower. There are quite a few tutorials online if you are interested in building one yourself. They take a bit of skill but aren't too complicated.

A second do-it-yourself option that is much more affordable is a Still Air Box (SAB). A SAB is comprised of a large, clear tote bin with holes cut into the sides for your arms. It is designed so you can reach into the box with your hands without opening the whole box. This greatly reduces the chance of opportunistic microbes from jumping in. The big beneficial part of this option is that they are inexpensive to make; a tote bin and utility knife to cut the holes is all that's needed. The bin also cleans up easily with alcohol wipes. It is recommended that the grower wears gloves as well while handling everything to make it even safer. Unfortunately, it can be very awkward to inoculate 5lb bags of substrate in the bin while only using your hands. This can be remedied a bit by creating smaller substrate bags and using a larger tote bin.

Some mushroom types aren't as susceptible to airborne contaminants as others. Oyster mushrooms, in particular, are quite adaptable and hardy. This isn't to say you should leave the substrate exposed to the air for long periods of time, however, it is possible to work fast and still be okay.

FIGHTING SUBSTRATE CONTAMINANTS

As described in the paragraph on sterilization and pasteurization, the substrates need to be treated before being inoculated to have a successful grow. If the substrate has been improperly sterilized or pasteurized, it will become contaminated. This is actually a common reason why mushrooms fail to grow. Take your time and do it right!

FIGHTING EQUIPMENT CONTAMINANTS

Any tub, stirring spoon, knife, and workspace should be wiped down completely with alcohol before any work with mushrooms is done. Don't neglect this step. Make sure all your tools are sterilized before you start working so you don't need to interrupt your process once you get started.

FIGHTING CULTIVATOR CONTAMINANTS

The cultivator is you! That's right, you are a huge source of potential contamination for your mushroom substrate. Hair, skin, dirty hands, dirty clothes, and even your breath can introduce a host of microorganisms that will ruin your inoculation.

It is highly recommended that you shower before you begin any inoculation process just to be sure. Be sure to clean your hands thoroughly since this is the main contact you will have with the substrate. Scrub under your fingernails and use lots of hand sanitizer. Latex gloves are a good addition too. Hospital or lab scrubs are commonly worn by growers. At the very least, try to wear freshly laundered clothes. A face mask is advised to keep your breath from contaminating your work.

To be successful in maintaining a sterile environment, it needs to be developed as a habit. It takes practice to always remember to scrub your hands or wear a mask. It also takes a focused mindset to pay attention to where potential contaminants might come from. If you touch something that is not sterile, even if you're wearing gloves, you will need to scrub your hands again and apply hand sanitizer.

It is also important to work quickly to reduce the exposure to the substrate. Once you open the bag or container of treated material, move as efficiently as possible. Don't rush because you don't want to make mistakes. But, be aware of what you are doing and how long it will take to be done. Moving efficiently and doing everything in a predetermined order reduces the overall time it will take for you to complete the inoculation. The more often you do it, the quicker it will become second nature and the success of your inoculations will be greatly increased.

SIX IMPORTANT METHODS FOR A STERILE GROWING ENVIRONMENT

1. Step one: keep your area clean! You will want to dedicate a workspace to mushroom cultivation. Clean the area completely. It will need to be close to the kitchen, as the sterilization procedures will occur there in most cases. There's little point in creating a sterile room if you're just going to take materials from the kitchen through a spore-infested area to the workroom. Your workroom should have a good-sized table to house your working materials, and this table should be covered with laminated plywood or thick vinyl so that it can be cleaned easily.

2. You'll also want to avoid carpets in the workroom, as they tend to house millions of spores. Make sure that the floors are easy to clean and that you can readily spot any dirt or other contaminants. The same will go for the walls of your workspace. You may even wish to give the walls a fresh coat of paint (latex is best) so that you can reduce the likelihood of initial contaminants and clean them regularly. Clean and disinfect the kitchen and workspace. If possible, use organic, orange-oil-based disinfectants.

3. Try to keep the workspace free of drafts and random air movement. If necessary, close all windows and air conditioning ducts. Try to keep the door closed and let air settle before working with your cultures. You may wish to work with glove boxes or laminar flow hoods to reduce the

likelihood of contamination from airborne bacteria and spores.

4. Air filtration for your workspace is recommended as well. If using flow hoods or air filtration, you'll want to use a HEPA-rated filter. Keep the filter on low at all times, and run it on high for at least an hour before working on your cultures. You'll also want to keep your workspace free of pets, potted plants, pet's food bowls, litter boxes, or any other sources of organic contaminant.

5. Personal hygiene is extremely important. There's no point in maintaining a clean space if you're just going to contaminate it with millions of mold spores from your clothing and body. Shower off before working on your culture. Dry yourself with a clean towel, and put on clean clothes just before attending to your cultures. Tie back long hair. Avoid loose-fitting clothing. Clean your hands and forearms with rubbing alcohol before beginning work, and use disposable surgical gloves (also cleaned with rubbing alcohol) to reduce the risk of contamination.

6. Consider mental hygiene as well. You'll want to use slow, steady movements that disturb the air as little as possible. Try to avoid urgency or distraction. Being focused, present, and unrushed will bring the best results. It's best to avoid distraction. Keep people out of the room when you're working at the least, and at all times if possible. If you like

music when you're working, go for soothing stuff that helps you to maintain focus and keep things steady. Remember, small mistakes can lead to contamination and make entire cultures unusable.

CREATING A "GLOVE BOX"

Essentially, a glove box is a small enclosure designed to allow you to work with your spawn with minimum exposure to the contaminants that might be present in your workspace. It will work best when you have taken every effort to create a clean workspace, as it's impossible to completely eliminate the risk of contamination.

Glove boxes are relatively simple and inexpensive to build, and the materials you need for them are easy to obtain. They should be used if there is the slightest risk that your cultures will be exposed to contamination. They will vastly increase the success of your cultivation efforts. There are many ways to build one, but the easiest is probably to use a transparent plastic container with a lid.

Materials

- Plastic container
- Knife or rotary tool to cut through plastic
- PVC pipe–2 pieces with 4" diameter and 2"- 3" long
- Tube of silicone sealant
- Elbow length rubber gloves
- Hose clamps, zip ties or strong rubber bands to attach the gloves to the PVC pipes

Construction

1. Decide where the arm ports should be by working out where your arms will be most comfortable while working. Cut a 4" diameter hole for each arm, using a knife or rotary tool.

2. Insert the PVC pipes into the cut holes.

3. Leave about ½" of pipe sticking out of the box.

4. Apply sealant around the pipe on both the inside and the outside of the box and leave to set overnight.

5. Slide the gloves over the pipes inside the box. Check that left and right gloves are on the correct sides and that they are in a comfortable position for you.

6. Fasten the gloves onto the pipes.

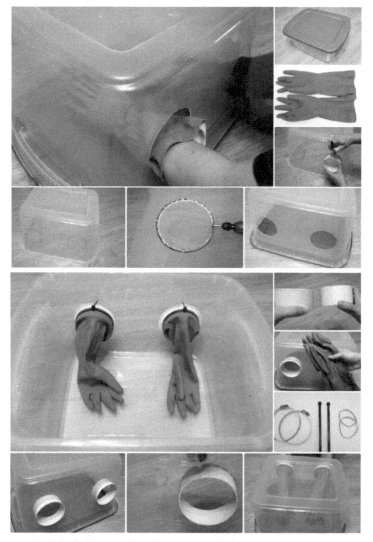

Jason Paul Smith/Instructables

What is important about a glove box is that sterile techniques must be applied before each use and after every time that the seal is broken. This means wiping down all surfaces, spraying an alcohol or disinfectant spray into the air inside and around the box, and rubbing gloves with alcohol before you commence work.

Right...now at last, we can get down to actually growing some of those wonderful mushrooms.

That's it! You now have a glove box that you can use to work with your materials in sterile conditions. You can collapse the box and store it easily when it's not in use, and the contact paper allows you to disinfect the surfaces before you start working with your cultures. The downside of the glove box is that it's not large enough to work with several jars or more than one spawn bag. It also won't completely eliminate the risk of contamination, but it will substantially reduce the likelihood of it.

When working with the glove box, use small hand motions to avoid stirring up more air than necessary. Wipe the inner surface of the box with alcohol to sterilize prior to use. After placing your materials in the box, spray a fine mist of 10% bleach solution to disinfect the air and outer surfaces of your working materials. Allow it to settle for at least 5 minutes before beginning your work.

Let the flaps drape over your arms as you work. Do not lift the lids of your jars further or for longer than necessary, and try to keep the lid above the opening of the jar or bag. Finally, seal all jars and bags securely before removing them from the glove box.

RECORD KEEPING

This part is essential if you wish to take your cultivation journey past a few batches. In many cases, you will cultivate certain strains and fungal lines. Plus, you'll want to know what conditions work best and any situations that lead to contamination or other challenges. You will want to mark the cultures so that you can easily identify the lines. This will also help you to monitor your progress. Note the strain, the substrate, the day of work, and the elapsed time for the batch. Over time, you'll likely create codes that indicate the originating strain and number of the current experiment, as well as the conditions that favor or interfere with fruiting.

CHAPTER 7:

DIFFERENT GROWING METHODS

The most tried and true mushroom-growing processes are outlined for you below. Each one tells you what tools you will need, how to set up your substrate, and how long to wait. There are many options for growing even one kind of mushroom. For example, the Oyster mushroom can be grown using all these techniques except the compost blend. On the other hand, the Button mushroom can only be grown using the compost blend. Next to each method, I have indicated which mushrooms should be grown using it. So, while you are thinking about what you want to grow, also think about how you want to grow it. That is, if it's a mushroom that has a variety of options.

GROWING IN STRAW BAGS (OYSTERS, ENOKITAKE)

-Indoor Method-

Straw is a popular growing substrate because it is inexpensive, provides excellent nutrition, and is easy to break down, which makes it easy to use. Mushrooms will not struggle to grow in a substance like straw; they can break through it easily when they are ready to fruit. These instructions assume you already have spawn available to use. If you do not, please see the above chapter to learn about inoculating your own spawn or how to purchase it ready-made. Make sure you are using straw and not hay, there is a difference!

Straw can be obtained from a local farm or farm supply store. Some places sell already-pasteurized straw although I think I'd still pasteurize it just to be sure. It doesn't cost too much for a bale and goes a long way to creating growing substrate.

What you will need:

- Mushroom spawn
- Straw, enough to fill several plastic oven bags (or larger)
- Large cooking pot
- Water
- Thermometer
- Nylon mesh bags or laundry basket
- Rubber gloves
- Strainer
- Plastic bags (like oven bags or bigger, depending on how much you are growing)
- A sharp, clean knife
- Twist ties

DECIDING HOW MUCH STRAW TO USE

This isn't an exact science. Generally, a 1:5 ratio of spawn to straw is a good place to start. So, if you have 1 pound of spawn, you will need to pasteurize 5 pounds of straw. Use this calculation to figure out how much straw and how many plastic bags you will need.

STEP 1 - PASTEURIZATION

Pasteurization is used to eliminate as many microscopic competitors as possible in the straw. Any competing organisms will use up nutrients that the fungi could use to flourish and may cause a crop to fail.

There are a variety of methods to pasteurize straw. Here, I will explain the hot water method, since it is easiest and can be scaled up or down easily depending on how much straw you have. Pasteurization happens between 70-80 °C/160 – 180 °F. Temperatures higher than this can kill good bacteria so it is important to maintain the correct range. The straw needs to soak in the hot water bath for at least an hour to be pasteurized.

The first step in pasteurization is to cut the straw into very small pieces, 1-3 inches long. Do not skip this! Yes, it's tedious but if you don't do it, it will take longer for your mushrooms to grow. Fungi colonize shorter pieces of straw a lot easier and this will diminish the wait time for fruiting. It will make a difference, believe me! If you have a small amount of straw to cut, you should use a blender or food processor. Larger batches can be put through a wood chipper or run over a bunch with a lawnmower. Do not do it by hand unless you like super sore fingers.

Fill a large pot, or any container that will fit the straw, with hot water and bring it to a boil. When it reaches a boil, turn down the heat by about one third and start checking the temperature. A meat thermometer works well here. When the temperature stays stable in the 70-80 °C/160-180 °F range, then it is ready for the straw to be added. It is likely you will need to play around with the heat a bit to get it to this point, but be patient and it will get there.

Put your straw in the nylon mesh bag and submerge it in the water. Put something heavy on top of the straw or pot to ensure all the straw is immersed. Because it is so light, the straw might try to bob out of the water a bit and then those pieces won't be properly pasteurized.

Let the straw sit for an hour, making sure to keep an eye on things, especially the temperature. After an hour, very carefully remove the straw. It will be hot! Rubber gloves come in handy here. Place the bag in a strainer and let it cool completely. Cooling completely is extremely important because too much heat will kill the spawn you are about to mix in. Once cooled, the straw needs to be used immediately.

STEP 2 – INOCULATION

Lay the cooled straw out in a box, on a clean table, or tarp. Break up the spawn and mix it into the straw until it is well combined. There isn't a scientific method to this, just mix it all up as thoroughly as possible.

Fill each plastic bag with the straw. Pack it in well, but not so tight that it is compressed. Close the top of each bag with a twist tie, forcing as much air out of the top of the bag as possible. Poke holes in the bag with the sharp knife every three or so inches. This is where the mushrooms will grow out.

STEP 3 – SET UP

The bags should be hung in a cool, dark place to facilitate the mycelium incubation. A good temperature for most species is 15-23 °C/60-75 °F. Make sure you read up on the spawn you are using and know what temperature it needs.

STEP 4 – WAIT

This is the fun part! Or the way that you learn the joys of patience. During this time, do not disturb the bags. They do need to be checked for moistness on a regular basis. If you see the straw is dry, mist it with a spray bottle through the holes.

The mycelium will colonize the straw in 2-8 weeks, again depending on variety, strain, and conditions. Check to see what the expected time is for the spawn you are growing.

The mushrooms should start to appear soon afterward. If they do not, the fruiting can be initiated through the addition of a bit of light. Not direct light! A low light, like the type you can use to read, is enough.

STEP 5 – HARVEST!

As soon as the mushrooms have grown large enough to harvest, pick them. It is usually best to pick individual ones as they are ready, instead of waiting for them all to be ready at the same time. Mushrooms can go funky fast so it's best to pick them at the peak of ripeness.

It's likely you can get more than one fruiting from a bag, so when it is done the first time, water the straw again and put them back in darkness. Check back regularly to see if the mycelium is fruiting again.

Notes and Reminders

- The mycelium of Oyster mushrooms and many others is white. Double check what the color of your mushroom mycelium should be. Large patches of red, black, brown, blue, and green mean the presence of mold. In this case, as absolutely devastating as it is, discard the bag. Any mushrooms grown in mold could make you sick and we want to avoid that!

- The mycelium needs to be kept wet without being soggy. This can be a fine balance. Check it regularly and if it is dry, as I said before, spray water through the holes. If there is water gathered in a pool at the bottom of the bag, poke some more holes and drain it out.

Picture 26: Growing on Straw. Watcharakorn Narbandit/Shutterstock.com

OPTIONS WITH STRAW

1. Instead of using plastic bags you can use clear **poly tubing or mushroom grow bags** to hold the spawn/straw mix. This will make much larger bags, so only do this if you have the space and if you have stronger arms. The use of poly tubing is preferred by many because you have more control over the size of the bags, it is tougher, and it provides a greater surface area for growing.

2. A **five-gallon bucket** is a fun and easy container to grow Oyster mushrooms in. This mushroom is the best choice for the method since it is the least sensitive. To prep a five-gallon bucket, drill 10 holes, spaced about 6 inches apart, in a staggered manner around the center section of the bucket.

Fill it with the prepared straw/spawn mix. Cover the top with a loose-fitting plastic bag. Cut 10 -12 holes in the top of the plastic bag to allow air flow. Continue the remainder of the process the same as with a bag, maintaining appropriate temperatures and moisture until fruiting occurs.

GROWING IN COFFEE GROUNDS | COCO COIR | VERMICULITE (OYSTER)

- Indoor Method-

The method described here uses coffee grounds, however exactly the same preparation technique is used for growing on Coco Coir and vermiculite. I have provided notes at the end of this chapter specific to the Coco Coir and vermiculite mix.

This is by far the easiest way to grow mushrooms. As long as you have access to a large amount of coffee grounds, you can do this. Time to make friends at your local coffee shop! Seriously, ask them if they will save their grounds for you – in a couple days, you'll likely have way more than you need. This method is only recommended for Oyster mushrooms.

This method is preferred by many because of its simplicity and the ease with which it can be set up. Also, it's extremely inexpensive and uses waste material that would normally fill the trash or compost. Re-use is the best!

There is some debate over whether it is best to add straw to the coffee grounds to create a more nutritious substrate for the mushrooms. Growers have had success both ways, using only coffee grounds and using a mix of coffee grounds and straw. The biggest problem with using only coffee grounds occurs when you are filling large bags or containers. The ground can become quite compacted and not provide the air flow that is necessary for mushroom growth.

Adding straw breaks up the substrate a bit and gives the mushrooms better air access.

The only real downside to adding the straw is that it increases the time needed to prepare the substrate for growing. For this guide, I am detailing how to grow on just coffee grounds and then at the end, there are instructions on how to add in straw if you would like.

What you will need:
- Mushroom spawn
- Coffee grounds
- 5-gallon bucket
- Drill and drill bit
- Straw (optional, see notes at end)

DECIDING HOW MUCH COFFEE GROUNDS ARE NEEDED

Growers agree that a 1:10 mixture of mushroom spawn to coffee grounds is a good guideline.

STEP 1 – ACQUIRE COFFEE GROUNDS

Coffee grounds are the granular remains of coffee leftover from brewing. Since they have been through the hot brewing process, they are already pasteurized. Depending on how many containers you intend to set up, you could need a lot of grounds. The local coffee shop is best for this.

The coffee grounds MUST be inoculated the same day they are brewed, because if they are allowed to sit, mold and other unwelcome organisms will make themselves at home. If you are gathering from a coffee shop, ensure that they are starting with a fresh bucket for you that doesn't include previous days' grounds or anything like that. Alternately, the grounds can be stored in a freezer until they are ready to use. The cold stops any growth from happening. Then, when you are ready to inoculate, bring them to room temperature before adding the spawn.

If you are saving the coffee grounds from your house, it will probably take a while to gather enough for growing. In this case, put a bag or bucket in your freezer and add the grounds to it every day until you have enough. Do not let them accumulate somewhere outside the freezer since that will encourage mold to grow.

If you are unsure of the pasteurization of your grounds, you can pasteurize them yourself. Place the grounds in a clean linen bag and place them in a pot of hot water. The water should be brought up to between 70-80 °C/160-180 °F and then the heat turned off. Let them soak for 1 ½ hours. When they are done soaking, very carefully remove the bag from the pot and set it, bag and all, in a strainer to cool.

STEP 2 – PREPARING THE BUCKET

In this method, we are using a 5-gallon bucket to hold the inoculated substrate. Plastic bags can also be used. Drill (4) 1/2"-3/4" holes around the center of the bucket. This is where the mushrooms will grow out.

STEP 3 – INOCULATION

Combine the (defrosted) coffee grounds and mushroom spawn in a clean 5-gallon bucket. Use a large clean spoon to mix it all together until it is well combined. The mixture should fill the bucket 2/3 full so that the mycelium has ample air available. Shake or thump the bucket gently, or agitate it, to get rid of any air pockets. Cover the bucket with its lid, but not tightly, or use tinfoil to cover the top.

STEP 4 – WAITING

Place the bucket in a warm, dark location. It should be warm day and night. Mist the coffee grounds through the holes in the bucket every few days, or as needed, to make sure they don't dry out.

After 7-14 days, you should see a white fuzzy growth stretching across the coffee grounds. This is the mycelium taking hold. When the coffee grounds are fully covered with white patches, move the bucket to a place where there is some indirect light (not direct sunlight!) so the mushrooms can begin fruiting. Remove the lid from the bucket at this stage.

In 5-12 days, you will see the little baby mushrooms popping out of the substrate. Continue to spray them daily to ensure they are getting enough moisture.

STEP 5 – HARVEST!

When the caps of the Oyster mushrooms begin to flatten, then they are ready to be harvested. Cut the cluster off with a sharp knife.

After harvesting, continue to mist the coffee ground substrate as another fruiting should happen in a few weeks.

OPTIONAL ADDITION OF STRAW

Straw must be pasteurized before being added to the coffee grounds. See instructions in the growing on straw method for how to do straw pasteurization. The formula for spawn, coffee grounds, and straw is 10% spawn to the weight of coffee grounds and 20% straw for the weight of coffee grounds.

COCO COIR/VERMICULITE MIX

Coco Coir is the ground up husks of coconuts and vermiculite is an organic soil amendment. They are both easily sourced and inexpensive to buy. These two growing substrates can be mixed in a 1:1 ratio to create an amazing growing medium for mushrooms. The Coco Coir and vermiculite need to be pasteurized before being used.

Coco Coir comes in dehydrated blocks and needs to be hydrated. Use the pasteurization technique listed below for cardboard. Put the Coco Coir and vermiculite in a bucket, pour boiling water over it, and let it sit. Use the amount of water that the Coco Coir package says is needed to hydrate it.

If you like, you can also add in a couple handfuls of pasteurized coffee grounds for added nutrition and nitrogen. Your mushrooms will thank you. Continue on with the process as you would with coffee grounds.

GROWING ON CARDBOARD (OYSTER)

-Indoor Method-

This is another grow method for Oyster mushrooms. Oysters, it seems, can grow on just about anything. You can try other mushrooms using this method, however, I could not comment on the success of it. The use of waste material (cardboard) in this method makes it a great choice for environmental purposes. Using waste to grow food is awesome!

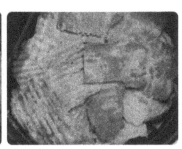

For this method, you simply need to collect some clean cardboard and get some spawn. It doesn't get much easier. You can also use cardboard egg trays.

What you will need:
- Mushroom Spawn
- Clean cardboard
- Plastic containers – any size you like, from quarts to gallons.
- Bucket or container to hold cardboard during pasteurization.
- For this method, use 20% spawn to cardboard.

Step 1 – Prepare your cardboard/Pasteurization

Remove all tape, staples and labels from your cardboard so it is just the cardboard material. Cut or rip it into pieces that will easily fit into your plastic container of choice.

Place the cardboard in a bucket that has a lid and is large enough to hold all the cardboard. An old ice cooler works really well for this. Boil enough water to cover all the cardboard. Pour the water into your bucket and place a weight of some sort on top of the top piece of cardboard to keep it weighted down and entirely covered in water.

Put the lid on the bucket and let it sit for a minimum of eight hours. Let it cool completely. The cardboard is now pasteurized and ready for the next step.

While the cardboard is pasteurizing, poke several small holes in the bottom of your plastic container for water drainage.

Step 2 – Inoculation

Drain away as much water as you can from the cardboard. Squeeze the cardboard to get rid of any excess water. Make sure you are wearing gloves or that your hands have been scrubbed before handling the cardboard.

Place a layer of cardboard in the bottom of your plastic container. Spread some spawn on top and then repeat it like a layer cake – cardboard, spawn, cardboard, spawn, cardboard. Make sure you end with cardboard at the top.

STEP 3 – WAITING AND CARETAKING

Place a large plastic bag, like a clear garbage bag, over the plastic container – use whatever type of plastic bag that will encompass the whole container. Close it up.

Put the container in a warm, dark place. Check it to make sure no water is pooling at the bottom. Excess water will encourage bad molds to grow.

Let the mushrooms colonize for 3-6 weeks. Don't forget about them! When the white mycelium has covered all the cardboard, it is ready to move onto the fruiting stage.

STEP 4 – FRUITING

The cardboard should be entirely covered with white mycelium. If it is not, put it back in the dark space until it is.

Open the bag so there is airflow to the colonized cardboard. This will be the sign to the mushrooms that it is time to fruit. Move the container, in its bag with the top open, to a place where there is a small amount of non-direct light. The rule of thumb is that there should be just enough light to read by.

Twice a day, mist the cardboard with water. Try not to spray the mushrooms directly as this will encourage some molds to grow. Spray the inner walls of the bag so the moisture drips down and creates a nice level of humidity.

STEP 5 – HARVESTING

For Oyster mushrooms, harvest them before the edges get wavy. They are still good when the edges are wavy, however, they are in their perfect prime just before.

Continue spraying the mushrooms with water 1-2 times per day and keep them in the light location. A second flush of mushrooms should appear in 10-15 minutes. Keep spraying after the second flush and you may get a third or fourth as well.

"LASAGNA" MULCHING FOR GROWING

(WINE CAPS, ENOKITAKE, OYSTER)

-Outdoor Method-

This is an outdoor method that works wonderfully for a number of mushroom types, including Wine Cap, Enokitake, and Oyster varieties. This method requires that you have some outdoor space suitable for setting it up. The space should be partially shaded or have full shade.

The best season to start a bed of Wine Caps is the beginning of spring. The fall, 30-40 days before the first frost, is also good. It is important not to let the beds dry out.

Use fresh wood chips! Freshly chopped the day you are inoculating. After they are allowed to sit for more than a day, other organisms and microbes will invade and your mycelium will have to fight for resources.

Wine Caps can grow on just straw, cardboard, or wood chips. When they grow on just straw, they use up the nutrients quicker and the harvest is smaller in size with smaller mushrooms. Using only wood chips means it will take much longer for the mycelium to fruit. Wood chips, though, will produce large, meaty mushrooms for a longer period of time then straw. The lasagna method combines the best of both worlds.

What you will need (for a 10x10 space):

- 5lb bag Mushroom spawn

- (1) Yard fresh hardwood chips

- Cardboard (enough for a double layer over your space)

STEP 1 – SET UP THE BED

Place a single layer of cardboard over the entirety of your garden bed. Spread 2-3 inches of wood chips on top of the cardboard.

STEP 2 – "LASAGNA"

Sprinkle half the spawn on top of the wood chips, crumbling it up well as you spread it. Next, add another layer of wood chips; again 2-3 inches is good. Then, add the rest of the spawn. After you've made your layers, place a single layer of cardboard on top of your pile. Water the cardboard really well.

STEP 3 – THE WAIT

Water the garden every day for 2 weeks then let it be. If there are particularly dry times or droughts in your area, water the bed when it's looking dry.

Wine Caps will take anywhere from 6-12 months to fruit. Be patient!

STEP 4 – HARVESTING

When you can just see the gills and the stem breaks easily, harvest the Wine Caps. They grow fast and get bitter when they are too large. Watch out for other little animals who would very much appreciate a snack – you want to get there before they do!

STEP 5 – YEARLY MAINTENANCE

Each year, add 1-2 inches additional fresh wood chips on top of your garden bed.

ALTERNATE "LASAGNA" RECIPE

Another recipe for the lasagna layers is to use hardwood chips and straw instead of the cardboard. For this method, start with a 2" layer of wood chips. Over the wood chips spread a layer of straw. Over the straw, spread the mushroom spawn. Repeat the layers – wood chips, straw, spawn – one more time. Finally, spread a 1" layer of wood chips over the top and water it well. Keep it moist and well-watered for several weeks.

GROWING ON SUPPLEMENTED HARDWOOD SAWDUST

(OYSTERS, SHIITAKE, LION'S MANE, MAITAKE, ENOKITAKE)

- Indoor Method-

A by-product of the lumber industry, hardwood sawdust is a versatile growing medium. It is favored by many growers because so many kinds of mushrooms can grow in it and you can get fantastic yields. This method isn't technically difficult; however, it does require some additional equipment and know-how than when using straw substrate. The sawdust needs to be sterilized (different from pasteurization) which requires having and using a pressure cooker.

Use sawdust from hardwoods like oak, beech, hickory, and maple, or a mix of those. Do not use sawdust from softwoods (spruce, fir, pine) because they are not good for growing mushrooms. To make the substrate, the sawdust is usually mixed with wood chips to provide a better structure for the growing mycelium. On its own, the sawdust is a bit too fine.

Sawdust can be acquired directly from the lumber mill or from your friends' wood-cutting pile. If neither of those are an option, however, hardwood pellets are available at most home supply stores. The pellets are what are used for wood stoves so look in that area of the store. Depending on where you live, they may be a seasonal item. If you can't find them at a store, they are available online. Pellets need to be soaked before use to create sawdust.

Picture 27: Growing on Hardwood Sawdust. Wade Machin/Shutterstock

The sawdust is supplemented with a nutritional nitrogen-rich addition. The choices for this include oat bran, wheat bran, millet, ground corn, spent barley left over from beer brewing, and rice bran. The supplement is added to quicken the growth of the fungi since they are slow at digesting the sawdust. They will grow fine without the addition of a supplement; however, it will take longer. The downside to adding the supplement (there always is one, right?) is that the mycelium will be expended quicker and the second and third flushes from your substrate will be smaller.

What you will need:

- Hardwood sawdust or pellets (1 cup pellets = approximately 3 cups sawdust)
- Spawn
- Mixing bucket
- Pressure cooker
- (2) 5lb Autoclavable grow bags (able to withstand the heat of a pressure cooker)
- 1.5 quarts water
- Oat bran
- A few small squares of Tyvek material for the filter

STEP 1 – MIX THE SAWDUST

The recipe for this substrate is quite simple and makes enough for two 5lb sawdust logs. It is recommended to make several recipes at a time. The amount you need will depend on how much spawn you have and what can fit in your pressure cooker. This recipe is enough for 1.5 lbs. of mushroom spawn.

10 cups hardwood pellets + 1.5 quarts water + 2 cups oat bran

Slowly, add the water to the hardwood pellets in a large bucket, tote bin, or container. Do it incrementally as you don't want the whole thing to be soggy. The pellets should look like loose sawdust. You may not need all the water. Using warm water makes the process go a little quicker, however cold water works well too. This may take a bit of time. Be patient and make sure all the pellets are broken down.

Add the oat bran to the sawdust and mix thoroughly. Fill your plastic bags with the mixture. Place a square of Tyvek over the sawdust and then fold the ends of the plastic bag in the way the product instructs. The Tyvek acts as a filter after you've taken the bags out of the pressure cooker and prevents contaminants from sneaking in while the bags cool.

STEP 2 – STERILIZATION

Before you place the bags in the pressure cooker, line the bottom of the cooker with canning jar lids or something metal and thin. This is to prevent the bags from touching the bottom of the cooker and burning.

Stack the bags on top of each other in the pressure cooker. Add water to the pressure cooker to just below the top of the bottom bag. Add a heavy plate on top of the bags so they don't move around and potentially clog the pressure valve. Cook at 15 PSI for 2 ½ hours.

Allow the blocks to cool for a minimum of 8 hours. Hot substrate will kill mycelium. They can stay right in the pressure cooker until you are ready to use them.

STEP 3 – INOCULATION

Carefully open up the bags and add 12-14 ounces spawn per bag. Use a large sterilized spoon to mix it all up really well. If you have made your bags bigger or smaller, then the amount of spawn added will change. Use the recipe above to determine how much.

Re-close the bags and tie off the tops with a zip tie or band.

STEP 4 – THE WAITING PROCESS

Place the bags in a warm, dark location. It should be warm day and night. After 10-30 days, you should have mycelium spreading all throughout the bags. The length of time will depend on what type of mushroom you are growing. Check on it daily or every other day to monitor the progress.

Once the mycelium has spread, move the bags to their fruiting location. The place you choose for this will depend on the type of mushroom you are growing. Most will need a warm space with a minimal bit of indirect light to start the fruiting process. The spawn you purchased should indicate the optimal fruiting temperature.

For Shiitakes, when the block is fully colonized, leave it until it forms a brown outer crust and large knots. The knots will protrude out like big bulbs. This phase is commonly referred to as "popcorning". Next, shock the mycelium by exposing it to cold temperatures (8-10°C/37-40°F) for 12-24 hours. A freezer will work, as will a refrigerator, or depending on where you live, outside could work well too. After the shocking, place the sawdust block in the fruiting area for growth. When the baby mushroom pins begin to show, remove the plastic bag.

Open the top of the bags and let them sit again. Keep them with just the top open. The fruiting process can take 5-15 days, usually. Again, it depends on the type of mushroom and the strain. Soon enough though, you should see little mushroom pins forming.

STEP 5 – HARVESTING!

When the mushrooms reach the size you want, carefully cut them off by the stem. Treating the hardwood sawdust block nicely is important so you can get 2-3 more fruitings out of it.

ALTERNATE HARDWOOD SAWDUST SUBSTRATE

76% Sawdust, 12% millet, 12% bran with a 65% moisture ratio. For one 5lb sawdust block, this translates to 1.5lb sawdust, .23lb millet, .23lb bran, and 46 ounces water.

GROWING IN BOTTLES

(ENOKITAKE, MAITAKE, OYSTER)

-Indoor Method-

Using bottles to grow mushrooms is a traditional method perfected in particular by Japanese cultivators. Don't forget, polypropylene mushroom bags have not been around forever! Bottles are used in growing Enokitake to get a special shape and size. Maitake and Oyster mushrooms are often grown in bottles too. In large operations, the bottle technique ends up being more efficient and cost-effective which makes it very attractive. There are a number of downsides too, of course.

Growing mushrooms in bottles appeals to many because it allows you not to rely so heavily on plastic. Single-use plastic can add up fast and will contribute to the growing garbage landfill problem we have in this world. Bottles are re-usable and recyclable. That is a huge bonus! Using bottles is an environmentally friendly choice. Additionally, mushrooms grown in bottles have very consistent forms and fruits, making them easier to harvest and to sell.

The main downside to growing mushrooms in bottles is the limited species that you can do it with. Using plastic mushroom grow bags allows for much more variety. Even though the mushrooms grown using the bottle technique are uniform and highly desirable in form, they are smaller than mushrooms grown using a grow bag. Simply enough, they just don't have as much space to spread out.

The time it takes for the mycelium to colonize the bottles is longer than with grow bags. Sometimes up to 2 weeks longer. But patience is a virtue, right? The final downside to growing in bottles is that you can only get one flush of mushrooms from them. There is not enough substrate to host a second one. Bag-grown mushrooms, on the other hand, can usually produce 2-3 flushes.

The easiest type of jar for the home-grower to use is a glass mason jar, or any pint or quart size glass jar. You can also use high-density polyethylene plastic bottles.

What you will need:

- Mushroom spawn
- Quart size Mason jars or other glass jars, with lids
- All the ingredients for (1) Recipe Hardwood Sawdust Substrate (see above for the recipe)
- A large tub
- Poly-fil stuffing (like stuffed toy animals are made with)
- A metal paper punch
- Cheesecloth (enough to cover the tops of all the jars)
- Plain white paper & tape

STEP 1 – PREPARE THE JAR LIDS

Using the paper punch, punch two holes in the metal jar lid. They should be on opposite ends of the lid, about 3/4" in from the edges. Take 2 small pieces of the poly-fil stuffing and push one into each hole so that there is some on the inside and outside and it is secure. The poly-fil should make a relatively tight seal.

STEP 2 – PREPARE THE SUBSTRATE

Combine the ingredients for the substrate in a large tub. Mix and hydrate them until you have a relatively dry, crumbly sawdust-like mixture. Fill the jars with the substrate up to a 1/2" from the top. Bang the jars one by one on a hard surface to knock out any air pockets.

Using the handle of a round spoon, like that of a wooden spoon, approximately 3/4" in diameter, make a hole in the center of the substrate. The hole should go all the way to the bottom of the jar. This is where the spawn will go after the jars are sterilized. Put the lids back on the jars.

STEP 3 – STERILIZATION

Place the jars **upright** in the pressure cooker. Placing them on their sides will cave in all the holes you just worked to create. Handle the jars gently to keep the holes intact. Set the pressure cooker at 15 PSI for 120 minutes.

STEP 4 – INOCULATION

After the pressure cooker has cooled, the jars are ready to be inoculated. Be careful to keep a sterile environment! Unscrew the lid and pour the mushroom spawn into the center hole in each jar. Replace the lid, sealing it tightly.

STEP 5 - WAITING

Place the jars in a secure location away from any direct sunlight. Room temperature should be fine, but be sure to double-check the mushroom species you are growing to ensure you have optimal conditions.

The spawn can take 3-4 weeks to grow. Once it does, wait for it to take over all the substrate before moving them to a fruiting location. Once the mycelium is covering all the substrate, move the bottles to ideal fruiting conditions for that mushroom (it will vary by species).

STEP 6 - FRUITING

Take the lid off the jar and place a wet layer of cheesecloth over it. This will maintain the humidity of the jar. When the cloth dries, spritz it with water. Keep a close eye on the jar. Once the mushrooms start pinning, you will need to remove the cheesecloth to give them space to grow out the top of the jar.

STEP 7 – HARVESTING

Cut the mushroom's stems off across the top of the jar.

STEP 8 – RE-USE

Clean those jars out and use them again. And again!

Picture 28: Growing in Bottles. Kietsuda Katkasem/Shutterstock.com

GROWING ENOKITAKE IN BOTTLES – SPECIAL INSTRUCTIONS

Enokitake are grown to look way different than they do in the wild. To get the long, spindly stems, the mycelium is inoculated in glasses or plastic bottles and a sleeve is inserted to control the growth. This way, when the pins start to grow, they are limited in horizontal space and so they grow long and tall straight upwards.

The Enokitake isn't difficult to grow, even though it has an extra step unlike other mushroom types. Enokitake need cool temperatures to prosper, not warm temperatures like most mushrooms. Enokitake can be grown on straw and on hardwood sawdust substrates. Allowed to grow free-form on those materials, they will look more like a regular mushroom. With this technique, they will grow long and thin like the ones that are found at the supermarket.

There are two changes to the process as described above if you want tall, thin Enokitake mushrooms. Both these changes happen after the mycelium has colonized the substrate. The first thing is to place the colonized jars some place where the temperature is around 10°C/50°F to fruit. Other mushrooms want warm temperatures while Enokitake crave cold. They will still fruit in higher temperatures but it will take longer and they may not be as robust. At this point, they can actually be put in the refrigerator. That's how much they love cold!

The second alteration happens during the pinning stage. Once the mushrooms start to pin, remove the cheesecloth. Next, attach a paper cone around the lip of the mason jar. The cone can be any height you want, really, but 3-4" is a good place to start. You should have spindly, tall mushrooms growing up through the cone in a few days. The jars can still be kept in the refrigerator if you like. In fact, the Enokitake might prefer this.

COMPOST BLEND FOR GROWING

(BUTTON MUSHROOMS)

-Indoor or Outdoor Method-

Button mushrooms, as common as they are, require a special growing environment that differs from other mushrooms. They need lots of nitrogen and will not grow without some type of manure or compost to feed on, in addition to straw or mulch chips.

When you are growing these mushrooms, choose your space wisely. Compost stinks! A basement or crawl space is great. These can also be grown outdoors – instructions are provided after the indoor ones.

What you will need:
- Compost
- Peat Moss (enough to cover the top of tray)
- Grow tray, at least 8" deep and about 2'x4'
- Mushroom spawn
- Newspaper
- Spray bottle

You will need about 2 cups of mushrooms spores for an 8-foot square of space. Scale this method to suit your needs.

Notes about Compost

The compost you use should be wet without being soggy. You should not be able to see any water dripping out. To test it, squeeze a small amount between your thumb and forefinger. The optimal compost should release 2-3 drops of water and that is it.

Many garden centers and online retailers sell compost specifically for mushrooms. This is what you want. Because the Button mushrooms are using the compost as almost their sole source of nutrition, it is important that it has all the components needed.

Be sure you are getting compost FOR mushrooms and not mushroom compost. There is a huge difference. Compost for mushrooms is compost that has been built specifically to nourish mushroom mycelium and facilitate their growth. Mushroom compost is the spent substrate left over after mushroom growing. Many farmers like to use this as a rich addition to their fields and gardens.

You can use your own compost if you like, however you will need to pasteurize it beforehand. Straight compost from your kitchen won't do, either. It needs to be mixed with a nitrogen-rich material like horse manure, coconut coir or gypsum.

STEP 1 – SET UP & INOCULATION

Fill your tray with compost up to about 2 inches from the lip. Sprinkle the spores over the top of the compost. Mix it all up really well with a sterilized spoon.

Place the tray in a cool, dark, moist location like a basement. Mist the compost daily to keep it moist. It can take 1-3 weeks for the mycelium to appear.

STEP 2 – CARE AND WAITING

When the white mycelium begins to appear, cover the tray with a 2" thick layer of peat moss and then a layer of newspaper. Maintain a temperature around 65-70°F. Every day for two weeks, mist the top of the newspaper with water until it is damp.

When you see the mushrooms beginning to pin, remove the newspaper. Continue misting the top of the compost daily until you get mushrooms ready to harvest.

STEP 3 – HARVESTING

Here's the fun part. What kind of mushrooms do you want? Buttons or Portobellos? Cutting them when they are still small will give you button mushrooms. Letting them grow out to their full size will give you Portobellos. Whichever one you choose, harvest them by cutting them off at the bottom of their stems with a sharp, sterile knife.

When you are done harvesting, leave the substrate where it is and look for 2-3 more flushes to harvest over a period of 2-4 weeks.

OUTDOORS GROWING IN COMPOST

Growing outdoors requires the set-up of a bed of some sort. A raised bed garden is perfect for this. You can also create one out of logs, wood, or concrete blocks. The ideal bed size is 4 feet x 4 feet x 8 inches. You can always make the beds bigger in length and width but try to keep the height the same.

Picture 29: Growing on Compost. Kuttelvaserova Stuchelova/Shutterstock.com

As you did with the indoor tray, fill the garden bed with approximately 6" of compost. Cover the compost with cardboard and then a layer of black plastic sheeting. Fasten the sheeting plastic firmly to the sides of the bed. This creates a sterilization chamber for the soil. Let it sit like this for two weeks.

When the two weeks is up, remove the plastic and the cardboard. Spread the mushroom spores over the compost and mix it in really well.

Spread the peat moss over the compost after you see the white mycelium appear. Cover the peat moss with newspapers and mist it daily with water to keep everything moist. Do this for 10 days. When the mushrooms appear, remove the newspaper and continue the daily misting. Harvest them as you do the indoor ones. Keep an eye out for additional flushes in the weeks following the first flush. It is possible to get 2-3 more flushes from the bed.

Important Note: Any time you grow outside, you take the chance that other wild mycelium will take advantage of this optimal growing space and join your button mushrooms in the garden bed. Before you consume any mushrooms, be sure you identify them!

GROWING MUSHROOMS ON LOGS OUTSIDE (SHIITAKE, MAITAKE, LION'S MANE, OYSTER)

-Outdoor Method-

It takes some know-how and a bit of sweat to be successful at this method. However, if you love Shiitake or Maitake, have access to some hardwood logs, and want to jump into the world of forest mushrooms, this is a great place to start. Each log that is inoculated can produce around a pound of mushrooms and can fruit and flush for about 3 years. This makes the initial investment of time and energy well worth it!

Picture 30: Growing on Logs. Unicus/Shutterstock.com

It is highly recommended that you start with a just a few logs in the beginning. Shiitake grow in warm, moist environments on dead hardwood tree logs. Maitake mushrooms prefer specifically oak hardwood logs. The mycelium grows rapidly in warm temperatures and with high rainfall. Sudden changes in temperature and moisture cause the spawn to fruit and the mushrooms to grow. If you live in an area with high temperatures during summer months and limited rainfall, you will need to soak or water the logs on occasion to keep up the moisture content. Make sure to take this into consideration when you are planning where to set up your logs. Near an easy water source is ideal!

STEP 1 – THE LOGS

Shiitake and Maitake need hardwood logs. Oak is the best choice for longevity of production since they decompose slower than others; this gives the fungi an expanded time to fruit. Shiitake actually means "oak mushroom", and Maitake in the wild grows on oak most commonly. Red oak is considered the absolute best choice with white oak being a close second. Beech, cherry, birch, ash, sugar maple, and hickory logs will also work. They will not provide the same lifespan, however. Black locust should never be used because it has strong anti-fungal properties that will prevent growth.

Actually, all trees produce anti-fungal compounds, called coumarins, to prevent the parasitic mushrooms from killing them. The coumarins accumulate around any wound in the tree to fight off the intruders, so this means they will be strong where you cut the tree. As the logs age, the coumarins dissipate.

Harvest time of the logs is still a subject that is being discussed and experimented with. The general consensus is that logs should be cut from living trees in winter or early spring when the temperature during the day is in the 50's and temperatures at night are still freezing. The reason for this is because it is when the sap from the tree begins to move up from the roots and spread out. This makes an ideal food supply for any fungus. Some growers harvest their logs as late as October successfully. Logs should never be harvested during hot summer months. When the trees are cut, the bark will need to be kept dry and the moisture content of the log high until they are ready to be inoculated. If the trees are cut in late winter, let them lie intact for 10 days before cutting them into logs. They should then be inoculated within 90 days. If the trees are cut in spring, they should also lie intact for 10 days before cutting them into logs. They should be inoculated within 1 month but preferably within 2 weeks. If the trees have to be cut into logs at the time of felling, then make sure to inoculate them within 10 days.

When you harvest the number of logs you intend to inoculate, they will need to sit for a minimum of three days for the anti-fungal compounds to disperse. It is better to wait up to 1-2 weeks after cutting if possible, though. Choose log sections that are clean of any other fungi. Fungi are opportunistic! While you are attempting to create the perfect environment for your inoculation, other fungi are ready and waiting to take over if they can. The logs should be green. This means no other fungi or growth. Green wood is also ideal because it has a higher moisture content and will provide a food source to the mushrooms for a longer time frame.

Logs should be around 3-6 inches in diameter and 3-4 feet in length. This is for ease of handling. They can most certainly be bigger; however, you will find them difficult to move around which can be troublesome.

STEP 2 – THE SPAWN

Mushroom spawn is available online or you can ask a local fungi grower or expert where they source the spawn. The mycelium comes impregnated into wooden dowels, mixed with sawdust, or as a liquid. As mentioned previously, there are different strains available from different suppliers. Shiitake spawn is available in cold weather, warm weather, and wide-range strains. It is recommended to try all three to see which works best in your area.

The most popular choices for spawn are plugs and sawdust. Plugs are easier to use; however, sawdust has better mycelium colonization rates.

STEP 3 – INOCULATION

Whether using plugs or sawdust, the technique is basically the same. Holes will need to be drilled into the logs to place the spawn. Plugs will need holes 1 inch deep, drilled with a 5/16inch drill bit. Sawdust spawn will need a hole the same size as the sawdust plunger. Check with the spawn supplier to ensure exactly what will be needed.

In general, the commonly accepted inoculation method is to drill holes 3 inches apart in rows down the length of the log. There should be 3-4 inches in between rows. A staggered diamond pattern is the ideal since close spacing increases the speed of colonization.

Put the plugs or sawdust into the holes immediately after drilling to prevent other fungi from jumping in. Seal the holes with cheese-wax or paraffin, again, to keep the other fungi out and also the keep the spawn from drying out. For optimal growth, the moisture content needs to be around 35-55%. A wood moisture meter will help a lot in maintaining optimal growing conditions. If the moisture content goes below 25%, the spawn will die.

Soak the logs immediately after plugging them unless they were cut less than 10 days ago. Soak for 12-24 hours but no more than 24 hours.

STEP 4 – STORAGE & CARE

The logs will next need to be placed in a well-shaded area that is protected from the wind so they don't dry out. Stack them close to the ground and close together to conserve moisture as well. There needs to be space between the logs for air circulation. Many growers use a crisscross or box pattern to stack the logs. Slope-stacking is also popular. Choose a method that works well for your particular situation and makes care of, and harvesting of, the mushrooms as simple as possible.

And now comes the fun part: waiting! Spawn can take 6-18 months to incubate. This all depends on temperature, moisture content, the fungus strain, and how much spawn are in each log. This time of waiting for the mycelium to take hold is called the spawn run. Maitake spawn can take upwards of 3 years for the first fruiting.

Logs need to be watered on a regular basis if there is no rain. On average, they need a good soaking by rain at least once a week. If Mother Nature is not providing this, you will need to. This can be a huge pain if you are not set up near an easy water source! Logs should be soaked for 24-36 hours and this can be done in several ways. If you have tubs, tanks, or barrels that can fit the logs, then set them in there for the allotted time. Don't forget, wet logs are a lot heavier than dry logs! Alternately, you can set up some type of irrigation system or overhead watering system so they can be drenched in place without having to move them.

STEP 5 - HARVESTING

A sign that the spawn run has been successful is the appearance of mycelium on the ends of the logs. Usually, it is fuzzy and white, although it can also be brown. Left on their own, they will fruit naturally. However, if you want to induce fruiting, you can soak the logs for 24 hours (if there is no rain forecast) and mushrooms should appear within a week. You will know it was successful by the appearance of pins – tiny mushroom heads coming out of the wood.

Forced fruiting can be done every 4-8 weeks for a continual harvest. However, this reduces the number of years they will produce. The average log that has been forced to fruit will last 2-3 years and those allowed to fruit naturally will last 3-5 years.

Five to seven days after the mushroom first appears, it will be ready to be picked. Shiitake should be harvested daily during this time, to ensure they are being picked at their peak. The ideal appearance time is when there is still a small curl at the edge of the cap.

When the mushrooms are ready, gently break off them off at the stem and put them in cardboard boxes or paper bags. They can be kept refrigerated for two to three weeks. They will only be fresh for a few days at room temperature.

NOTES

1. Growing Lion's Mane on logs: It can take 1-3 years for this mushroom to produce. Using larger logs, at least 10" in diameter, will give you larger mushrooms. The logs should be partially buried vertically in the ground for best results.

2. Growing Maitake on logs: Partially bury logs horizontally. Only use oak logs.

CHAPTER 8:

MUSHROOM GROWING EQUIPMENT

This list of equipment is not needed for every grower or growing situation. Be sure to check the equipment needed for the growing method you are using.

GROW BAGS

The world of grow bags is quite fascinating and specific. These bags are useful for several reasons. They can be used to hold the substrate/spawn mixture for fruiting, making them a vital part of the mushroom growing process. They can also be used to hold substrate that needs to be sterilized.

Picture 31: Grow Bag. ArtCookStudio/Shutterstock.com

The so-called basic mushroom grow bag is technically known as a gusseted autoclavable polypropylene filter patch bag. Yes, that's right, say that five times fast! This bag has all the specialty design a grower could want. The gusseting explains how the bag is to be folded. The sides of the bag fold flat towards the inside. Autoclavable means the bag can withstand high temperatures, such as during the sterilization process for sawdust. Polypropylene refers to the material it is made of, a type of plastic that can hold up to those high temperatures. The filter patch is a filter on the front of the bag that allows the mushrooms to get fresh air in without pesky contaminants joining in.

Mushroom bags have different filter ratings, ranging from .2 microns to 5 microns. For fruiting uses, as explained in this book, you want one with a low micron rating. It shouldn't be higher than .5 microns to ensure protection from contamination while you are growing.

Bags are also available in different sizes. The size you need depends entirely on how much substrate you are using to fill it. The bag's description will usually indicate how many pounds of material it can hold.

PRESSURE COOKER

If you decide to use a method that requires sterilization of materials, you will need to get a pressure cooker. The type of pressure cooker is not that important, as long as it works. Look for one that is large enough for your anticipated needs as well.

Pressure cookers will either have a steam release valve or a weighted metal rocker. The sort with the rocker is best for canning. What you really want is the type that has a steam

release valve. These are called *Konjushenko Vladimir/Shutterstock.com* "stopcocks" and the pressure cookers which contain them are known as sterilizers. You'll need to pay plenty of attention to it, as it can explode if too much pressure builds up. At the same time, if you use a rocker-style pressure cooker, you'll need to watch it to make sure the liquids don't boil over and ruin your medium. In the long run, it's more than worth it to just get the stopcock-style cooker.

When using a pressure cooker, you'll want to make sure that no steam escapes from the seals. If you are using a metal-on-metal cooker and steam is escaping from the seals, turn off heat, allow it to cool, and run a bead of Vaseline around the seal. Make sure that there is at least ½" water in the cooker when heating, and never place items directly on the bottom or against the walls. Most pressure cookers will have a rack to position contents as needed.

Allow the cooker to heat slowly, and bring it to a full head of steam before closing the stopcock. Don't leave it unattended, especially in the early stages of heating when the heat and pressure fluctuate erratically. You'll want to check it every ten minutes or so. This will let you avoid over-pressurization and ensure that the proper temperature and pressure are maintained throughout the cycle so that the contents are fully sterilized.

Don't touch the cooker when it's going if you want to avoid a nasty and painful burn. Also, allow the pressure cooker to cool slowly when the heating is finished. Don't try to cool it more quickly with cold water. Uneven cooling can cause glass to break or the contents of the cooker to violently implode. Also, watch the steam from the stopcock. **It's hot!** Finally, to ensure sterile conditions, wrap the outlet of the stopcock with an alcohol-soaked cloth prior to opening the valve. This will ensure that no spores or other contaminants enter the cooker when you vent the steam.

Pressure cookers can be found pretty much anywhere, from second-hand shops to grocery stores to scientific shops and mushroom supply stores.

SPAWN

There are multiples of mushroom spawn providers online. Look for one with excellent reviews. Even better, talk to some mushroom folk in person or online and ask who they suggest. It is all too easy to get bad spawn and reputation is a big deal in this world. It would be awful to put in the effort of preparing your substrate, inoculating, and then waiting, and see no results because the spawn was no good to begin with. Do your research before buying!

STRAW

Straw is commonly available at farm and home stores or from your local farmer. Make sure you are getting straw and NOT hay. Look for clean straw without any obvious contaminants or dirt. If you do not live near a farmer or farm store, you can buy clean straw online through a variety of retailers. Look for clean, processed straw.

SAWDUST

As discussed earlier, hardwood sawdust is used to create a substrate that many mushroom species thrive on. It is important that the sawdust be fresh and only contain wood from hardwood trees.

MASON JARS AND LIDS

These are used in one grow method and are a great re-usable choice for growing. They're easy to find at supermarkets and are sturdy and can be re-used

Graham Taylor/Shutterstock.com

indefinitely. As far as lids go, you can use the two-piece metal lids used for canning, or the plastic lids that can be easily modified for gas exchange. You can use Ball "Storage Caps". These can be autoclaved and they will seal your culture from outside contaminants. To modify them, cut or drill a 1-inch hole in the center. Then, fit the lid with a filter disk so air can enter, but harmful contaminants are blocked.

JAR FILTER DISKS

These are sold at most online stores and mushroom growing shops. They are used for growing mushrooms in jars. The filtration lets air in without allowing in contaminants. They are to be used in place of poly-fil stuffing in the instructions provided for this technique. Both ways work well. The filter disks are of course cleaner and fancier, but then, more expensive. They are nice to have but not necessary unless you are finding you have a contamination issue.

Filter discs are flat circles of synthetic fiber, several millimeters thick and heat resistant. They can be sterilized in an autoclave or pressure cooker and re-used. You cover holes in the lids of your Mason jars or in your growing chambers with them so that you can block out contaminants while allowing gas exchange. They will discolor when in contact with substrate or mold spores. If this happens, then soak them in a quarter-strength bleach solution.

In a pinch, Tyvek can be used. It can be found in supply stores or for free from FedEx or the post office in the form of indestructible mailing envelopes. If you use Tyvek, cut it an inch wider than the mouth of the jar. Then use the metal screw portion of a typical lid to clamp the Tyvek over the mouth of the jar. You can sterilize it, but you should dispose of it after a few uses.

SHOT GUN FRUITING CHAMBER (SFGC) (AND HOW TO MAKE ONE)

This is a specially made place to put your mushroom bags or jars while they are fruiting. It provides a balance of fresh air and humidity just as the mushrooms like.

Picture 32: DIY Fruiting Chamber

This fruiting chamber is extremely easy to make. Basically, it is a large clear tote bin with holes all over it, with a few inches of wet perlite covering the bottom. The holes bring in fresh air and the wet perlite maintains humidity. Only use clear tote bins. The mushrooms need the natural light. A dark or colored tote will not allow the mushrooms to prosper. The ideal tote bin size is around 64 qt. This size allows for head space to place the bags in and for the mushrooms to grow. A bigger tote may have air circulation issues and a smaller tote may be too small to put anything in.

Perlite is used for this because it forms a large porous surface when it gets wet with lots of space to hold water. The water evaporates over time and creates the humidity. Use coarse perlite, not fine perlite, so it doesn't come right back out the holes you are going to drill.

To create this SGFC, drill evenly spaced 1/4" holes on all six sides of the tote bin – this includes the lid and the bottom. The holes should be in a 2" grid pattern. To make the holes evenly spaced, use a tape measure and marker to draw it out before drilling.

Once the holes are drilled, fill the bottom of the tote with 4-5" of damp perlite. The perlite needs to be washed several times before use to get rid of any dust that may clog the holes you just drilled. When you are done adding the perlite, place the new SGFC in an elevated space, meaning the bottom has to be up off the floor with air flow beneath it. This is key to using the fruiting chamber effectively. Air needs to enter through the holes in the bottom to make the system work.

While your blocks or bags or jars are in the fruiting chamber, open the top a couple times a day to let in fresh air. The holes don't bring in quite enough. However, if the holes are made bigger, then the humidity will be lowered, which isn't ideal either. The easiest thing to do is just open the lid for a minute twice a day and wave fresh air into the box.

After you wave in fresh air, the perlite will need to be checked to ensure it is still moist. Add moisture with a mister or spray bottle if necessary, avoiding spraying the mushroom block as much as possible. Adding too much water to the mushroom block may induce mold growth. Spraying the sides of the tote so the water drips down onto the perlite is a good method for doing this.

HUMIDITY TENT

This is usually a plastic structure that goes over the mushrooms as they colonize and fruit to maintain specific humidity levels. They can be opened to let air in or closed off to maintain temperature. They can be found at a variety of retailers.

HYGROMETER

Here is another way to maintain those all-important humidity levels. This tool measures the humidity of a space for you. You can set one up in your grow room and it will digitally display the

humidity. These are not *RNko7/Shutterstock.com* completely necessary for the new mushroom grower but they are nice to have and aren't too expensive, which makes acquiring one worth it. These are nice because they also tell you the room temperature which is something you need to keep an eye on as well.

ISOPROPYL ALCOHOL

Isopropyl alcohol is essential as a disinfectant for containers, hands, and surfaces. It is also a fuel for alcohol lamps. It can be easily obtained at grocery stores or pharmacies in 70% or 91% concentration. Either concentration is suitable for cultivation purposes. When using it to sterilize tools, remember that it is extremely flammable. You'll want to make sure that the alcohol has evaporated before exposing tools to flame.

BLEACH

Detergent-free laundry bleach is excellent for cleaning and disinfecting surfaces and tools. ¼-strength is ideal for this purpose, while a 10% dilution in a spray form is best for disinfecting air and surfaces.

SURGICAL GLOVES

Surgical gloves help to keep contaminants from the hands away from your cultures. Wipe hands and forearms down with alcohol before putting them on, and then wipe the outside of the gloves with alcohol as well. Allow the alcohol to evaporate before coming near flame.

CHAPTER 9:
POTENTIAL PROBLEMS AND
PREVENTION

I would love to tell you that growing mushrooms is entirely fool-proof, but sadly, that just can't be true. Any time you are growing something, there is the potential for problems. You can have some control over some of these problems, but with some there is not much you can do to fix it. I've compiled this list of common problems that plague mushroom growers; however, it by no means contains every type of problem possible. Luckily, I can give you ideas on how to lessen many of the problems, if not eradicate them completely.

COMMON PROBLEMS

INCORRECT MOISTURE LEVELS

Correct moisture levels are very important for mushroom growth. After all, they are mostly made up of water. In general, mushrooms like a moist environment. In the wild, they most often grow after rainy weather or near wet, swampy areas. The growing substrate should be slightly damp at all times, without being soggy. Too much moisture is also a problem, so make sure the substrate isn't dripping or sitting in pools of water. Too much moisture will lead to mold, which will take over your substrate and push out the mycelium. To keep the substrate moisture level damp, mist it with a spray bottle of water. This way you can really control how much you are adding. Of course, the correct moisture levels depend entirely on what mushroom you are growing and the growing method, so make sure you know what your specific type of mushroom needs.

NOT ENOUGH FRESH AIR

To grow properly, mushrooms need access to fresh air, especially during the fruiting process. Without fresh air, they will be stunted if they grow at all. Some growing methods don't include a fresh air exchange in the colonization process, which seems to be okay. However, tests showing colonization rates when there is a fresh air exchange indicate that it speeds up the colonization process significantly.

The problem with fresh air, of course, is that it carries microbes and organisms that can cause harm. If you put in a fresh air exchange during the colonization time, make sure it has a filter to keep out any competitors for the space. If you are using a method that doesn't call for a fresh air exchange, briefly opening the container once a day to air it out will help the process along.

CONTAMINATION

As discussed in a previous chapter, all things must be kept as sterile as possible. Spores and mycelium are fragile and need a lot of special attention to succeed. Please follow the guidelines listed in the chapter on sterilization to make sure you are giving the mushrooms the best chance possible to survive.

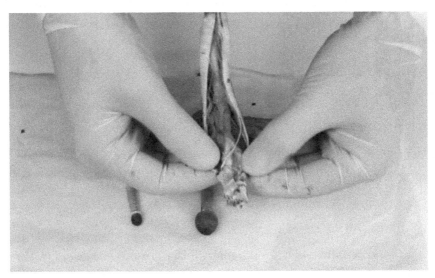

Picture 33: Contaminated Mushroom

BAD SPAWN/MYCELIUM

Unfortunately, there is not much you can do about this when it happens. And, unfortunately, there is no way to tell until you attempt to grow it. Since some mushrooms take so long to grow, it could be potentially years before you know the spawn wasn't good. The only way to avoid this is to make sure you only buy spawn from reputable companies. If possible, limit the amount of travel time the spawn has to get to you by buying locally or prioritizing shipping so it doesn't spend an exorbitant amount of time in transit.

PESTS & DISEASES

SLUGS (AND SNAILS)

This is more of a problem with outdoor growing. Slugs absolutely love mushrooms. If you are growing Shiitake on logs, you will need to keep an eye out for these slimy pests or they will help themselves to your entire harvest without even a thank you. When you see a slug, remove it immediately and check for others, because there certainly will be more. Check in the leaves and on the ground all around. If possible, elevate the logs off the ground so the slugs can't get to them quite as easily. There are a couple of products on the market that can kill slugs. Make sure you get one that is toxic only to slugs as you don't want to be killing every insect around; many are beneficial.

TURKEY TAIL

Another problem you will encounter in outdoor growing conditions, this troublemaker is actually another fungus. Turkey Tail is a decomposer, meaning it feeds on dying material. Logs are especially susceptible to this fungus invasion. Turkey Tail will push out the mycelium you are trying to grow and take the space all for itself. To reduce the chances of a Turkey Tail invasion, inoculate your logs quickly and use wax over the holes to prevent other organisms from sneaking in.

MAMMALS

Mice, squirrels, rabbits, and deer all love mushrooms as much as people do. If they find your mushroom-growing spot, they will surely help themselves to all your hard work. To keep mammals away, consider constructing fences, screens, or other barriers, and always harvest the mushrooms as quickly as possible.

MOLD

If you see mold growing on your substrate, throw out the block or bag immediately. Make sure to dispose of it far from your growing space. Once a growing medium is infected, it is highly unlikely the mycelium will survive, and you run the chance of it spreading to other mushroom growths. It is better to get rid of the bad one and hopefully save the others. Mushroom mycelium is almost always white. If you see any other color fuzz growing on your substrate, it is mold.

VERTICILLIUM SPOT

Mushrooms will look deformed and have spots on their caps. There will also be small dead areas on the cap. Verticillium spot is caused by a fungus and can be avoided through proper sterilization and sanitation management.

CHAPTER 10:

PROCESSING AND PREPARATION

STORING

Mushrooms are best used soon after harvesting. As soon as you pick them, they begin decomposing. To extend the shelf-life, all mushrooms can be refrigerated. Place them in a paper bag so they are protected, yet still have room to breathe. In general, it is best not to store them longer than a week, because even refrigerated, they will begin to break down and their quality will decrease.

DRYING

Mushrooms are really easy to dry since they are mostly water. Some species are better dried than others. Oysters, Buttons, Wine Caps, Shiitake, and Maitake are great dried. When you are ready to use them, they can be reconstituted before being added to a dish, or if you are making a stew, put them right in the cooking broth and they will re-hydrate. Lion's Mane dries well but the texture changes oddly when it is re-hydrated, so it is not recommended to dry Lion's Mane. Enokitake are so thin that they will practically disappear when they are dried. It is not worthwhile to dry them.

To dry mushrooms, clean them well and then let them rest on a layer of paper towels to get rid of any excess moisture. Lay them in a single layer in a dehydrator and set the temperature to medium. The time it takes will depend on the type of mushroom. Mushrooms can also be dried inside or outside if the temperature is warm enough to evaporate the moisture from them. To do this, clean them well and lay them to rest on a layer of paper towels to soak up moisture. When they no longer look soggy, remove them from the paper towels and place them in a single layer on a baking tray. Place the tray somewhere dry. Watch them carefully because if the location isn't dry enough, they can develop mold.

Mushrooms should be dried until they are hard as crackers. Store dried mushrooms in tightly sealed glass jars or plastic bags.

FREEZING

Since mushrooms are mostly water, freezing them raw does not work. The texture changes to a very unpalatable consistency when they are defrosted. Soggy mushrooms are not fun to eat! This does not mean mushrooms cannot be frozen, though. All it means is that they must be cooked first. Cooking (heat) will remove excess moisture and make them better candidates for freezing. Cooking them as part of a dish is the best method: for example, a Shiitake vegetable soup or an Oyster stir-fry.

If you cook them plain, be sure to drain off all moisture from the cooking process before freezing them. A good, general mushroom-cooking method is to dry sauté them until all their moisture is released, drain the moisture, and then add any fats, flavors, or seasonings that you wish. Freeze them in plastic freezer bags or freezer-safe containers.

CONCLUSION

It's a lot of information, I know! I hope you are feeling inspired and not overwhelmed. I promise, it gets easier after the first couple times. The number one rule of mushroom growing is to be prepared. You will have failures. It happens even to the best of mushroom growers. Following the instructions in this book, though, will help you avoid many of the mistakes that beginners make.

I am so excited for you to get out there and grow your own mushrooms. I hope you will tell me what you are growing and how it is going. I love hearing about successful harvests, and unsuccessful ones too, because then we can troubleshoot and hopefully prevent others from making the same mistake. We are all learning from each other so we can all be successful!

The variety of mushrooms available to grow makes this hobby so much fun. Experiment with the different types; maybe you'll discover a new favorite edible!

YOUR OPINION IS IMPORTANT TO ME

First of all, thank you for purchasing this book. I know you could have picked any number of books to read, but you picked this book and for that I am extremely grateful.

If you enjoyed this book and found some benefit in reading this, I'd like to hear from you and hope that you could take some time to post a review on Amazon. Your feedback really makes a difference to me.

If you'd like to leave a review all you need to do is to go to the book's product page on Amazon and click on *"Write a Customer Review"*

I wish you all the best for your fungi journey!

MORE BOOKS FROM
RICHARD BRAY

If you want to learn more about greenhouse gardening or growing food without soil, check out the other books in Richard Bray's book series on Amazon:

 **_GREENHOUSE GARDENING_**

How to Build a Greenhouse and Grow Vegetables, Herbs and Fruit All Year-Round

 **_DIY Hydroponics_**

12 Easy and Affordable Ways to Build Your Own Hydroponic System

 **_Hydroponics_**

How to Pick the Best Hydroponic System and Crops for Homegrown Food Year-Round.

ABOUT THE AUTHOR

Richard's father was a keen gardener and that is where his interest in all natural things began. As a youngster, he enjoyed nothing better than helping his father in the garden.

Nowadays, he finds himself at the opposite end of life. Having had a satisfying career, he now has time to potter around in his garden and take care of his small homestead. Much of the food on his dinner table is homegrown. He likes to experiment with various gardening methods and find new ways to grow bountiful crops year-round.

He wants to share his knowledge and show how easy and rewarding it is to set up your own prosperous garden. In his opinion, you don't need a huge budget to get started. When you do get started, you will soon feel, and taste, the benefits of growing your own food.

Learn more about Richard Bray at *amazon.com/author/richardbray*